W9-BMD-938

A Donald Justice Reader

The Bread Loaf Series of Contemporary Writers

DONALD JUSTICE

A Donald Justice
READER

SELECTED

POETRY AND PROSE

Middlebury College Press
Published by University Press of New England
Hanover and London

MIDDLEBURY COLLEGE PRESS
Published by University Press of New England,
Hanover, NH 03755
© 1991 by Donald Justice
All rights reserved
Acknowledgments appear on page 171
Printed in Canada   5   4   3

CIP data appear at the end of the book

Yet I do not doubt the existence somewhere—in the
atmosphere, let us say—of a sort of eternity of sounds.
I am told there are scientific grounds to believe this.
And in this eternity of sounds Eugene's rich, exact
notes persevere. They continue, they repeat themselves,
they endure—a form of energy, pure energy of the pure
spirit. I cannot hear them, or many of them, but I
believe they are there, like the laughter on old radio
shows or the conversations of Goethe, like the sword-
sounds of dim medieval battles or the dark surf
Homer himself heard without seeing.

—from the draft of a story

Contents

Contents

viii

Contents

A Bread Loaf Contemporary

A T A T I M E when the literary world is increasingly dominated by commercial formulas and concentrated financial power, there is a clear need to restore the simple pleasures of reading: the experience of opening a book by an author you know and being delighted by a completely new dimension of her or his art, the joy of seeing an author break free of any formula to reveal the power of the well-written word. The best writing, many authors affirm, comes as a gift; the best reading comes when the author passes that gift to the reader, a gift the author could imagine only by taking risks in a variety of genres including short stories, poetry, and essays.

As editors of The Bread Loaf Series of Contemporary Writers we subscribe to no single viewpoint. Our singular goal is to publish writing that moves the reader: by the beauty and lucidity of its language, by its underlying argument, by its force of vision. These values are celebrated each summer at the Writers' Conference on Bread Loaf Mountain in Vermont and in each of these books.

We offer you the Bread Loaf Contemporary Writers series and the treasures with which these authors have surprised us.

Robert Pack
Jay Parini

Author's Note

F R O M published work I have chosen writing I still like, or which others seem to. Mixed in are a few pieces, new and old, not reprinted before. All this has at best a sort of one-author unity, and it should be remembered that the author was several different persons during the course of writing, which covered many years.

The prose has been kept separate from the poems, but there is some crossover. The ending of one of the stories is retold as a poem, and the prose memoir is summarized twice over in a group of poems. In both cases the prose came first. Why this strikes me as logical I probably do not need to explain.

My poems are short, inevitably so, as it seems to me. There is only so much to be said on this or that subject, though I would like to think one may try the same subject from more than one angle. If Sherwood Anderson, one of my favorite writers, seems never to have had an idea longer than thirty or so pages, my own ideas come up even shorter. It is fair to say that I have so far remained unaffected by the American mania for epic. The truth is I would have written novels and five-act tragedies if I could have.

I am grateful to Robert Pack for suggesting the idea for this book.

P O E M S

Crossing Kansas by Train

The telephone poles
Have been holding their
Arms out
A long time now
To birds
That will not
Settle there
But pass with
Strange cawings
Westward to
Where dark trees
Gather about a
Waterhole this
Is Kansas the
Mountains start here
Just behind
The closed eyes
Of a farmer's
Sons asleep
In their workclothes

Poem to Be Read at 3 A.M.

Excepting the diner
On the outskirts
The town of Ladora
At 3 A.M.
Was dark but
For my headlights
And up in
One second-story room
A single light
Where someone
Was sick or
Perhaps reading
As I drove past
At seventy
Not thinking
This poem
Is for whoever
Had the light on

Henry James by the Pacific

In a hotel room by the sea, the Master
Sits brooding on the continent he has crossed.
Not that he foresees immediate disaster,
Only a sort of freshness being lost—
Or should he go on calling it Innocence?
The sad-faced monsters of the plains are gone;
Wall Street controls the wilderness. There's an immense
Novel in all this waiting to be done,
But not, not—sadly enough—by him. His talents,
Such as they may be, want an older theme,
One rather more civilized than this, on balance.
For him now always the consoling dream
Is just the mild dear light of Lamb House falling
Beautifully down the pages of his calling.

The Wall

The wall surrounding them they never saw;
The angels, often. Angels were as common
As birds or butterflies, but looked more human.
As long as the wings were furled, they felt no awe.
Beasts, too, were friendly. They could find no flaw
In all of Eden: this was the first omen.
The second was the dream which woke the woman.
She dreamed she saw the lion sharpen his claw.
As for the fruit, it had no taste at all.
They had been warned of what was bound to happen.
They had been told of something called the world.
They had been told and told about the wall.
They saw it now; the gate was standing open.
As they advanced, the giant wings unfurled.

for John Berryman

6

Sonnet to My Father

Father, since always now the death to come
Looks naked out from your eyes into mine,
Almost it seems the death to come is mine
And that I also shall be overcome,
Father, and call for breath when you succumb,
And struggle for your hand as you for mine
In hope of comfort that shall not be mine
Till for the last of me the angel come.
But, Father, though with you in part I die
And glimpse beforehand that eternal place
Where we forget the pain that brought us there,
Father, and though you go before me there,
Leaving this likeness only in your place,
Yet while I live, you do not wholly die.

South

I dont! I dont hate it! I dont hate it! —Q. COMPSON

*But why do I write of the all unutterable and the all
abysmal? Why does my pen not drop from my hand
on approaching the infinite pity and tragedy of all the
past? It does, poor helpless pen, with what it meets of
the ineffable, what it meets of the cold Medusa-face
of life, of all the life lived, on every side. Basta, basta!*
—H. JAMES

1. Porch

There used to be a way the sunlight caught
The cocoons of caterpillars in the pecans.
My boy-shadow would lengthen to a man's
Across the yard then, slowly. And if I thought
Some sleepy god had dreamed it all up—well,
There stood my grandfather, Lincoln-tall and solemn,
Tapping his pipe out on a white-flaked column,
And with the air of someone at his job.
(I liked to watch the pipe-stars as they fell.)
As for the quiet, some far train always broke it.
Then the great silver watch rose from his pocket,
And he would check the hour—the dark fob
Holding the watch suspended like a moon.
It would be evening soon then, very soon.

2. *Cemetery*

Above the fence-flowers, like a bloody thumb,
A hummingbird was throbbing. . . . And some
Petals took motion from the beating wings
In hardly observable obscure quiverings.
My mother stood there, but so still her clothing
Seemed to have settled into stone, nothing
To animate her face, nothing to read there—
O plastic rose O clouds O still cedar!
She stood that way for a long time while the sky
Pondered her with its great Medusa eye;
Or in my memory she did.
                                            And then a
Slow blacksnake, lazy with long sunning, slid
Down from its slab, and through the thick grass, and hid
Somewhere among the purpling wild verbena.

3. *Farm*

And I, missing the city intensely at that moment,
Moped and sulked at the window. I heard the first owl, quite near,
But the sound hardly registered. And the kerosene lamp
Went on sputtering, giving off vague medicinal fumes
That made me think of sickrooms. I had been memorizing
"The Ballad of Reading Gaol," but the lamplight hurt my eyes;
And I was too bored to sleep, restless and bored.
                                                    Years later,
Perhaps, I will recall the evenings, empty and vast, when
Under the first stars, there by the back gate, secretly, I
Would relieve myself on the shamed and drooping hollyhocks.
Now I yawned; the old dream of being a changeling returned.
The owl cried, and I felt myself like the owl—alone, proud,
Almost invisible—or like some hero in Homer
Protected by a cloud let down by the gods to save him.

4. *Train*

(Heading north through Florida, late at night and long
ago, and ending with a line from Thomas Wolfe)

Midnight or after, and the little lights
Glittered like lost beads from a broken necklace
Beyond smudged windows, lost and irretrievable—
Some promise of romance those Southern nights
Never entirely kept—unless, sleepless,
We might pass down the darkened aisle again
To stand, braced in a swaying vestibule,
Alone with the darkness and the wind—out there
Nothing but pines and one new road perhaps,
Straight and white, aimed at the distant gulf—
And hear, from the smoking room, the sudden high-pitched
Whinny of laughter pass from throat to throat;
And the great wheels smash and pound beneath our feet.

First Death

I saw my grandmother grow weak.
When she died, I kissed her cheek.

I remember the new taste—
Powder mixed with a drying paste.

Down the hallway, on its table,
Lay the family's great Bible.

In the dark, by lamplight stirred,
The Void grew pregnant with the Word.

In black ink they wrote it down.
The older ink was turning brown.

From the woods there came a cry—
The hoot owl asking who, not why.

The men sat silent on the porch,
Each lighted pipe a friendly torch

Against the unknown and the known.
But the child knew himself alone.

June 13, 1933

The morning sun rose up and stuck.
Sunflower strove with hollyhock.

I ran the worn path past the sty.
Nothing was hidden from God's eye.

The barn door creaked. I walked among
Chaff and wrinkled cakes of dung.

In the dim light I read the dates
On the dusty license plates

Nailed to the wall as souvenirs.
I breathed the dust in of the years.

I circled the abandoned Ford
Before I tried the running board.

At the wheel I felt the heat
Press upwards through the springless seat.

And when I touched the silent horn,
Small mice scattered through the corn.

June 14, 1933

I remember the soprano
Fanning herself at the piano,

And the preacher looming large
Above me in his dark blue serge.

My shoes brought in a smell of clay
To mingle with the faint sachet

Of flowers sweating in their vases.
A stranger showed us to our places.

The stiff fan stirred in mother's hand.
Air moved, but only when she fanned.

I wondered how could all her grief
Be squeezed into one small handkerchief.

There was a buzzing on the sill.
It stopped, and everything was still.

We bowed our heads, we closed our eyes
To the mercy of the flies.

Chorus

Slowly now from their dreams the sleepers awaken.
    And as, slowly, they grow aware of the light,
Which only by very gradual stages invades their rooms,
    Timidly at first, testing the sill,
And then more boldly, crossing the floor, regarding itself
Brightly in mirrors (which seem, indeed, to bloom,
Under such a gaze, like shy girls of the country,
    Or like small ponds that, dry all summer,
Brim all at once with the first rains of autumn)—
    It seems to them, half awake as they are,
That someone has left a light on for them,
    As a mother might for her children,
And that it has been burning there all night, quite close,
    Even while they were dreaming that they slept
In dark, comfortless rooms like these; or, in some cases, caves,
    Damp and airless; or a tunnel, extremely narrow,
Through which a train was expected momently, thundering.
    And the light left on seems to them perfectly natural,
And in fact necessary, for they have not yet remembered
    Who they are, and that they are no longer children.
And as, slowly now, they open their eyes to the light,
    It is in time to catch a glimpse of their dreams
Already disappearing around the last corner of sleep,
    The retreating tail of the monster winking and flashing.

from BAD DREAMS

Epilogue: To the Morning Light

O light,
Strike out across the pasture,
Where nightmare runs away now,
Unseating all her riders.
Show them the way through woods where
So recently they wandered,
Without direction. Shine, shine on those spiders'
Webs into which they blundered,
So many, recoiling with a gesture.

Dazzle the highways, paved
With fading journeys. And these walks
That lead into a town
From which the siege is lifting
Lace, lace with leaf-pattern now
Through the cooperation of the oaks
And a breeze constantly shifting.

Then leap the latched gate lightly,
O prodigal. Approach
This house, this anxious house your nightly
Exile fills with such gloom. How many chores
Await you! It is to you these stories
Declare themselves, all three now,
And at your glance how whitely!

Peer in through the tinted oval
There where the stair turns. No longer
Delay your necessary arrival.
But quickly, quickly
Stoop to the frayed runner
And follow it up the stair—
Steep, but less dangerous now that you
Go with it everywhere.

Reward each sleeper
With waking, with forgetting,

Your brilliant trophies.
Raise them up, but with care,
From pallets, from sprung sofas,
Where they have hung suspended
Over abysms, chasms,
Or drifted deep and deeper
Down through lost, bottomless pools.
See that their dreams are ended.

Teach them to forgive the mirror
Its frank, unfaltering look,
And the sundial in the side yard
Its shadow, for your sake.
For only with your help shall
They come to see—and with no more
Than average daily terror—
All things for what they are,
All things for what they are.

from BAD DREAMS

Children Walking Home from School
through Good Neighborhood

They are like figures held in some glass ball,
One of those in which, when shaken, snowstorms occur;
But this one is not yet shaken.
       And they go unaccompanied still,
Out along this walkway between two worlds,
This almost swaying bridge.
       October sunlight checkers their path;
It frets their cheeks and bare arms now with shadow
Almost too pure to signify itself.
And they progress slowly, somewhat lingeringly,
Independent, yet moving all together,
Like polyphonic voices that crisscross
In short-lived harmonies.

       Today, a few stragglers.
One, a girl, stands there with hands spaced out, so—
A gesture in a story. Someone's school notebook spills,
And they bend down to gather up the loose pages.
(Bright sweaters knotted at the waist; solemn expressions.)
Not that they would shrink or hold back from what may come,
For now they all at once run to meet it, a little swirl of colors,
Like the leaves already blazing and falling farther north.

Time and the Weather

Time and the weather wear away
The houses that our fathers built.
Their ghostly furniture remains—
All the sad sofas we have stained
With tears of boredom and of guilt,

The fraying mottoes, the stopped clocks . . .
And still sometimes these tired shapes
Haunt the damp parlors of the heart.
What Sunday prisons they recall!
And what miraculous escapes!

To the Unknown Lady Who
Wrote the Letters Found in the Hatbox

*To be sold at auction: . . . 1 brass bed, 1 walnut secretary . . . birdcages,
a hatbox of old letters . . .* —NEWSPAPER ADVERTISEMENT

What, was there never any news?
And were your weathers always fine,
Your colds all common, and your blues
Too minor to deserve one line?

Between the lines it must have hurt
To see the neighborhood go down,
Your neighbor in his undershirt
At dusk come out to mow his lawn.

But whom to turn to to complain
Unless it might be your canaries,
And only in bird language then?
While slowly into mortuaries

The many-storied houses went
Or in deep, cataracted eyes
Displayed their signs of want—FOR RENT
And MADAM ROXIE WILL ADVISE.

Memories of the Depression Years

1. *A Farm near Tifton, Georgia, c. 1930*

. . . in the kitchen, as she bends to serve,
Aunt Babe's too finely thin, upgathered hair
Filters the sunlight coming through behind
(Which is how Griffith lights his heroines).
Moth wings clïng to the door screen; dust motes whirl.
There is such a light!
              The grown-ups chatter on,
Unheard. Meanwhile I listen for the freight,
Due any minute. I can *see* the bell
Swing back and forth in close-up, silently,
The huge wheels revolving, the steam rising . . .
But already the silent world is lost forever.

2. *Boston, Georgia, c. 1933*

The tin roofs catch the slanting sunlight.
A few cows turn homeward up back lanes;
Boys with sticks nudge the cattle along.
A pickup whines past. The dust rises.
Crows call; cane sweetens along the stalk;
All around, soundlessly, gnats hover.
And from his stoop now my grandfather
Stands watching as all this comes to pass.

3. *Miami, Florida, c. 1936*

Our new house on the edge of town
Looks bare at first, and raw. A pink
Plaster flamingo on one leg
Stands preening by the lily pond.
And just as the sun begins to sink
Into the Everglades beyond,
It seems to shatter against the pane
In little asterisks of light,
And on our lids half-closed in prayer
Over the clean blue willowware.

Cinema and Ballad of the
Great Depression

We men had kept our dignity;
Each wore a cap or a hat. It seemed
We had become a line somehow;
Dark soup was all our dream.

We moved back in with parents. Some days
The awnings creaked like sails.
We lay upstairs on the bedclothes smoking
The long afternoons away.

Sometimes, folding the evening paper up,
One feels suddenly alone.
Yes. And down along the tracks by night
The slow smoke of nomad fires . . .

We slept; and over us a bridge
Arc'd like a promise. To the west
Nightglow of cities always then;
And somebody pulled out a harp.

Pulled a mouthharp out and played,
O lost and wordless . . .
And we were as numerous as leaves;
And some of us turned yellow, and some red.

Agriculture embraced Industry,
Mammothly, on public walls.
Meanwhile we camped out underneath
Great smiles on billboards fading.

And home might be some town we passed—
The gingerbread of porches scrolled
In shadow down the white housefronts;
And townboys playing baseball in a road.

Things will go better one day, boys.
Don't ask when.
A decade hence, a war away.
O meet me in the Red Star Mission then!

Pulled out an ancient mouthharp and began to play.

A Winter Ode to the Old Men of Lummus Park, Miami, Florida

Risen from rented rooms, old ghosts
Come back to haunt our parks by day,
They crept up Fifth Street through the crowd,
Unseeing and almost unseen,
Halting before the shops for breath,
Still proud, pretending to admire
The fat hens dressed and hung for flies
There, or perhaps the lone, dead fern
Dressing the window of a small
Hotel. Winter had blown them south—
How many? Twelve in Lummus Park
I counted, shivering where they stood,
A little thicket of thin trees,
And more on benches turning with
The sun, wan heliotropes, all day.

O you who wear against the breast
The torturous flannel undervest
Winter and summer, yet are cold,
Poor cracked thermometers stuck now
At zero everlastingly,
Old men, bent like your walking sticks
As with the pressure of some hand,
Surely they must have thought you strong
To lean on you so hard, so long!

Childhood

J'ai heurté, savez-vous, d'incroyables Florides. —RIMBAUD

Time: the thirties
Place: Miami, Florida

Once more beneath my thumb the globe turns—
And doomed republics pass in a blur of colors . . .

       Winter mornings then my grandfather,
Head bared to the mild sunshine, liked to spread
The Katzenjammers out around a white lawn chair
To catch the stray curls of citrus from his knife.
Chameleons quivered in ambush; wings
Of monarchs beat above bronze turds, feasting.
             And there were pilgrim ants
Eternally bearing incommensurate crumbs
Past slippered feet. There,
In the lily pond, my own face wrinkled
With the slow teasings of a stick.
            The long days passed, days
Streaked with the colors of the first embarrassments.
And Sundays, among kin, happily ignored,
I sat nodding, somnolent with horizons.
         Myriad tiny suns
Drowned in the deep mahogany polish of the chair arms;
Bunched cushions prickled through starched cotton . . .

              Already
I knew the pleasure of certain solitudes.
I could look up at a ceiling so theatrical
Its stars seemed more aloof than the real stars;
And pre-Depression putti blushed in the soft glow
Of exit signs. Often I blinked, re-entering
The world, or caught, surprised, in a shop window,
My ghostly image skimming across nude mannequins.
Drawbridges, careless of traffic, leaned there
Against the low clouds—early evening . . .

All day

There was a smell of ocean longing landward.
And, high on his frail ladder, my father
Stood hammering great storm shutters down
Across the windows of the tall hotels,
Swaying. Around downed wires, across broken fronds,
Our Essex steered, bargelike and slow.

Westward then

The smoky rose of oblivion bloomed and hung;
And on my knee a small red sun-glow, setting.
For a long time I felt, coming and going in waves,
The stupid wish to cry. I dreamed . . .

And there were

Colognes that mingled on the barber's hands
Swathing me in his striped cloth Saturdays, downtown.
Billy, the midget haberdasher, stood grinning
Under the winking neon goat, his sign,
As Flagler's sidewalks filled. Slowly
The wooden escalator rattled upward
Toward the twin fountains of a mezzanine
Where boys, secretly brave, prepared to taste
The otherness trickling there, forbidden.

And then the warm cashews in cool arcades!

O counters of spectacles!—where the bored child first
Scanned new perspectives squinting through strange lenses;
And mirrors, tilted, offered back toy sails
Stiffening breezeless toward green shores of baize . . .

How thin the grass looked of the new yards!
And everywhere

The fine sand burning into the bare heels
With which I learned to crush, going home,
The giant sandspurs of the vacant lots.
Iridescences of mosquito hawks

Glimmered above brief puddles filled with skies,
Tropical and changeless. And sometimes,
Where the city halted, the cracked sidewalks
Led to a coral archway still spanning
The entrance to some wilderness of palmetto—

Forlorn suburbs, but with golden names!

Dedicated to the poets of a mythical childhood—
Wordsworth, Rimbaud, Rilke, Hart Crane, Alberti

Absences

It's snowing this afternoon and there are no flowers.
There is only this sound of falling, quiet and remote,
Like the memory of scales descending the white keys
Of a childhood piano—outside the window, palms!
And the heavy head of the cereus, inclining,
Soon to let down its white or yellow-white.

Now, only these poor snow-flowers in a heap,
Like the memory of a white dress cast down . . .
So much has fallen.
                    And I, who have listened for a step
All afternoon, hear it now, but already falling away,
Already in memory. And the terrible scales descending
On the silent piano; the snow; and the absent flowers abounding.

Nostalgia of the Lakefronts

Cities burn behind us; the lake glitters.
A tall loudspeaker is announcing prizes;
Another, by the lake, the times of cruises.
Childhood, once vast with terrors and surprises,
Is fading to a landscape deep with distance—
And always the sad piano in the distance,

Faintly in the distance, a ghostly tinkling
(O indecipherable blurred harmonies)
Or some far horn repeating over water
Its high lost note, cut loose from all harmonies.
At such times, wakeful, a child will dream the world,
And this is the world we run to from the world.

Or the two worlds come together and are one
On dark, sweet afternoons of storm and of rain,
Of stereopticons brought out and dusted,
Stacks of old *Geographics*, or else, through rain,
A mad wet dash to the local movie palace
And the shriek, perhaps, of Kane's white cockatoo.
(Would this have been summer, 1942?)

By June the city seems to grow neurotic.
A lake serves very well then for reflection,
And ours is famed among painters for its blues,
Yet not entirely sad, upon reflection.
Why sad at all? Is their wish so unique—
To anthropomorphize the inanimate
With a love that masquerades as pure technique?

O art and the child were innocent together!
But landscapes grow abstract, like aging parents.
Soon, soon the war will shutter the grand hotels,
And we, when we come back, must come as parents.
There are no lanterns now strung between pines—
Only, like history, the stark bare northern pines.

And after a time the lakefront disappears
Into the stubborn verses of its exiles
Or a few gifted sketches of old piers.
It rains perhaps on the other side of the heart;
Then we remember, whether we would or no.
—Nostalgia comes with the smell of rain, you know.

Nostalgia and Complaint of the Grandparents

Les morts
C'est sous terre;
Ça n'en sort
Guère. —LAFORGUE

Our diaries squatted, toadlike,
On dank closet ledges.
Forget-me-nots and thistle
Decalcomaned the pages.
But where, where are they now,
. All the sad squalors
Of those between-wars parlors?—
Wax fruit; and the sunlight spilt like soda
On torporous rugs; the photo
Albums all outspread . . .
The dead
Don't get around much anymore.

There was an hour when daughters
Practiced arpeggios;
Their mothers, awkward and proud,
Would listen, smoothing their hose—
Sundays, half past five!
Do you recall
How the sun used to loll,
Lazily, just beyond the roof,
Bloodshot and aloof?
We thought it would never set.
The dead don't get
Around much anymore.

Eternity resembles
One long Sunday afternoon.
No traffic passes; the cigar smoke
Coils in a blue cocoon.
Children, have you nothing
For our cold sakes?
No tea? No little tea cakes?
Sometimes now the rains disturb
Even our remote suburb.
There's a dampness underground.
The dead don't get around
Much anymore.

Monologue in an Attic

[Enter ARTHUR, *a man of about 30, through a trapdoor.]*
The sad aroma of mothballs—
What a beautiful smell that is!
But where can the flies have got to
Now, that used to buzz at the pane
All summer, making their music?
I used to sit here admiring
Those ridiculous, long-drawn-out
Wagnerian death agonies
Of theirs for hours; once in a while,
One might stand up and stretch his wings,
Revived like the heldentenor
By demands for an encore.

             [A buzzing of flies is heard.]
                    Strange,
How nothing ever seems to change
Up here but the weather. Downstairs,
My mother's radio would be
Tuned to another opera.
Mother had tempests. Still, one could
Always escape to the attic. . . .

                    [Speech from a play] c. 1958

Ode to a Dressmaker's Dummy

*Papier-mâché body; blue-and-black cotton
jersey cover. Metal stand. Instructions included.*
—SEARS, ROEBUCK CATALOGUE

O my coy darling, still
You wear for me the scent
Of those long afternoons we spent,
The two of us together,
Safe in the attic from the jealous eyes
Of household spies
And the remote buffooneries of the weather;
So high,
Our sole remaining neighbor was the sky,
Which, often enough, at dusk,
Leaning its cloudy shoulders on the sill,
Used to regard us with a bored and cynical eye.

How like the terrified,
Shy figure of a bride
You stood there then, without your clothes,
Drawn up into
So classic and so strict a pose
Almost, it seemed, our little attic grew
Dark with the first charmed night of the honeymoon.
Or was it only some obscure
Shape of my mother's youth I saw in you,
There where the rude shadows of the afternoon
Crept up your ankles and you stood
Hiding your sex as best you could?—
Prim ghost the evening light shone through.

In the Attic

There's a half hour toward dusk when flies,
Trapped by the summer screens, expire
Musically in the dust of sills;
And ceilings slope toward remembrance.

The same crimson afternoons expire
Over the same few rooftops repeatedly;
Only, being stored up for remembrance,
They somehow escape the ordinary.

Childhood is like that, repeatedly
Lost in the very longueurs it redeems.
One forgets how small and ordinary
The world looked once by dusklight from above . . .

But not the moment which redeems
The drowsy arias of the flies—
And the chin settles onto palms above
Numbed elbows propped on rotting sills.

Thinking about the Past

Certain moments will never change, nor stop being—
My mother's face all smiles, all wrinkles soon;
The rock wall building, built, collapsed then, fallen;
Our upright loosening downward slowly out of tune—
All fixed into place now, all rhyming with each other.
That red-haired girl with wide mouth—Eleanor—
Forgotten thirty years—her freckled shoulders, hands.
The breast of Mary Something, freed from a white swimsuit,
Damp, sandy, warm; or Margery's, a small, caught bird—
Darkness they rise from, darkness they sink back toward.
O marvellous early cigarettes! O bitter smoke, Benton . . .
And Kenny in wartime whites, crisp, cocky,
Time a bow bent with his certain failure.
Dusks, dawns; waves; the ends of songs . . .

Manhattan Dawn (1945)

There is a smoke of memory
That curls about these chimneys
And then uncurls; that lifts,
Diaphanous, from sleep

To lead us down some alleyway
Still vaguely riverward;
And so at length disperses
Into the wisps and tatters

That garland fire escapes.
—And we have found ourselves again
Watching, beside a misty platform,
The first trucks idling to unload

(New England's frost still
Unstippling down their sides).
                    Or turned
To catch blue truant eyes upon us

Through steam that rose up suddenly from a grate . . .
                    Grinning—
And the grin slid off across the storefronts.
Dawn always seemed to overtake us, though,

Down Hudson somewhere, or Horatio.
—And we have seen it bend
The long stripes of the awnings down
Toward gutters where discarded flowers

Lay washing in the night's small rain—
Hints, glimmerings of a world
Not ours.
                    And office towers
Coast among lost stars.

Body and Soul

1. Hotel

If there was something one of them held back,
It was too inadvertent or too small
To matter to the other, after all.

Afterwards they were quiet, and lay apart,
And heard the beating of the city's heart,
Meaning the sirens and the street-cries, meaning,
At dawn, the whispery great street-sweeper cleaning
The things of night up, almost silently.

And all was as it had been and would be.

2. Rain

The new umbrella, suddenly blowing free,
Escaped across the car hoods dangerously.
And we ran after it—
                    only to be lost
Somewhere along the avenues, long avenues
Toward evening pierced with rain; or down some mews
Whose cobbles once perhaps the young Hart Crane
Had washed with a golden urine mixed with rain.

3. Street Musician

A cold evening. The saxophonist shivers
Inside his doorway and ignores the givers
Dropping their change into his upturned hat.
High now or proud, he leans back out of that,
Lifting his horn in some old bluesy riff
His fingers just do manage, being stiff—
Yet so sincere, so naked that it hurts.
Punk teens, in pink hair-spikes and torn T-shirts,
Drift past; a horse-cop towers above the cars;
And office lights wink on in place of stars.

Silence of cities suddenly and the snow
Turning to rain and back again to snow . . .

Tremayne

1. *The Mild Despair of Tremayne*

Snow melting and the dog
Barks lonely on his bottom from the yard.
The ground is frozen but not hard.

The seasonal and vague
Despairs of February settle over
Tremayne now like a light snow cover,

And he sits thinking; sits
Also not thinking for a while of much.
So February turns to March.

Snow turns to rain; a hya-
cinth pokes up; doves returning moan and sing.
Tremayne takes note of one more spring—

Mordancies of the armchair!—
And finds it hard not to be reconciled
To a despair that seems so mild.

2. *The Contentment of Tremayne*

Tremayne stands in the sunlight,
   Watering his lawn.
The sun seems not to move at all,
   Till it has moved on.

The twilight sounds commence then,
   As those of water cease,
And he goes barefoot through the stir,
   Almost at peace.

Light leans in pale rectangles
   Out against the night.
Tremayne asks nothing more now. There's
   Just enough light,

Or when the streetlamp catches
   There should be. He pauses:
How simple it all seems for once!—
   These sidewalks, these still houses.

3. *The Insomnia of Tremayne*

The all-night stations—Tremayne pictures them
As towers that send great sparks out through the dark—
Fade out and drift among the drifted hours
Just now returning to his bedside clock;
And something starts all over, call it day.
He likes, he really likes the little hum,
Which is the last sound of all nightsounds to decay.

Call that the static of the spheres, a sound
Of pure inbetweenness, far, and choked, and thin.
As long as it lasts—a faint, celestial surf—
He feels no need to dial the weather in,
Or music, or the news, or anything.
And it soothes him, like some night-murmuring nurse,
Murmuring nothing much perhaps, but murmuring.

4. *Tremayne Autumnal*

Autumn, and a cold rain, and mist,
    In which the dark pineshapes are drowned,
And taller poleshapes, and the town lights masked—
A scene, oh, vaguely Post-Impressionist,
    Tremayne would tell us, if we asked.

Who with his glasses off, half-blind,
    Accomplishes very much the same
Lovely effect of blurs and shimmerings—
Or else October evenings spill a kind
    Of Lethe-water over things.

"O season of half forgetfulness!"
    Tremayne, as usual, misquotes,
Recalling adolescence and old trees
In whose shade once he memorized that verse
    And something about "late flowers for the bees . . ."

A Dream Sestina

I woke by first light in a wood
Right in the shadow of a hill
And saw about me in a circle
Many I knew, the dear faces
Of some I recognized as friends.
I knew that I had lost my way.

I asked if any knew the way.
They stared at me like blocks of wood.
They turned their backs on me, those friends,
And struggled up the stubborn hill
Along that road which makes a circle.
No longer could I see their faces.

But there were trees with human faces.
Afraid, I ran a little way
But must have wandered in a circle.
I had not left that human wood;
I was no farther up the hill.
And all the while I heard my friends

Discussing me, but not like friends.
Through gaps in trees I glimpsed their faces.
(The trees grow crooked on that hill.)
Now all at once I saw the way—
Above a clearing in the wood
A lone bird wheeling in a circle,

And in that shadowed space the circle
Of those I thought of still as friends.
I drew near, calling, and the wood
Rang and they turned their deaf faces
This way and that, but not my way.
They stood upright upon the hill.

And it grew dark. Behind the hill
The sun slid down, a fiery circle;
Silent, the bird flew on its way.
It was too dark to see my friends.
But then I saw them, and their faces
Were leaning above me like a wood.

Round me they circle on the hill.
But what is wrong with my friends' faces?
Why have they changed that way to wood?

Sestina on Six Words by Weldon Kees

I often wonder about the others
Where they are bound for on the voyage,
What is the reason for their silence,
Was there some reason to go away?
It may be they carry a dark burden,
Expect some harm, or have done harm.

How can we show we mean no harm?
Approach them? But they shy from others.
Offer, perhaps, to share the burden?
They change the subject to the voyage,
Or turn abruptly, walk away,
To brood against the rail in silence.

What is defeated by their silence
More than love, less than harm?
Many already are looking their way,
Pretending not to. Eyes of others
Will follow them now the whole voyage
And add a little to the burden.

Others touch hands to ease the burden,
Or stroll, companionable in silence,
Counting the stars which bless the voyage,
But let the foghorn speak of harm,
Their hearts will stammer like the others',
Their hands seem in each other's way.

It is so obvious, in its way.
Each is alone, each with his burden.
To others always they are others,
And they can never break the silence,
Say, lightly, *thou*, but to their harm
Although they make many a voyage.

What do they wish for from the voyage
But to awaken far away
By miracle free from every harm,
Hearing at dawn that sweet burden
The birds cry after a long silence?
Where is that country not like others?

There is no way to ease the burden.
The voyage leads on from harm to harm,
A land of others and of silence.

Here in Katmandu

We have climbed the mountain.
There's nothing more to do.
It is terrible to come down
To the valley
Where, amidst many flowers,
One thinks of snow,

As, formerly, amidst snow,
Climbing the mountain,
One thought of flowers,
Tremulous, ruddy with dew,
In the valley.
One caught their scent coming down.

It is difficult to adjust, once down,
To the absence of snow.
Clear days, from the valley,
One looks up at the mountain.
What else is there to do?
Prayer wheels, flowers!

Let the flowers
Fade, the prayer wheels run down.
What have these to do
With us who have stood atop the snow
Atop the mountain,
Flags seen from the valley?

It might be possible to live in the valley,
To bury oneself among flowers,
If one could forget the mountain,
How, never once looking down,
Stiff, blinded with snow,
One knew what to do.

"]

Meanwhile it is not easy here in Katmandu,
Especially when to the valley
That wind which means snow
Elsewhere, but here means flowers,
Comes down,
As soon it must, from the mountain.

Women in Love

It always comes, and when it comes they know.
To will it is enough to bring them there.
The knack is this, to fasten and not let go.

Their limbs are charmed; they cannot stay or go.
Desire is limbo: they're unhappy there.
It always comes, and when it comes they know.

Their choice of hells would be the one they know.
Dante describes it, the wind circling there.
The knack is this, to fasten and not let go.

The wind carries them where they want to go,
Yet it seems cruel to strangers passing there.
It always comes, and when it comes they know
The knack is this, to fasten and not let go.

Variations for Two Pianos

There is no music now in all Arkansas.
Higgins is gone, taking both his pianos.

Movers dismantled the instruments, away
Sped the vans. The first detour untuned the strings.
There is no music now in all Arkansas.

Up Main Street, past the cold shopfronts of Conway,
The brash, self-important brick of the college,
Higgins is gone, taking both his pianos.

Warm evenings, the windows open, he would play
Something of Mozart's for his pupils, the birds.
There is no music now in all Arkansas.

How shall the mockingbird mend her trill, the jay
His eccentric attack, lacking a teacher?
Higgins is gone, taking both his pianos.

There is no music now in all Arkansas.

for Thomas Higgins, pianist

Villanelle at Sundown

Turn your head. Look. The light is turning yellow.
The river seems enriched thereby, not to say deepened.
Why this is, I'll never be able to tell you.

Or are Americans half in love with failure?
One used to say so, reading Fitzgerald, as it happened.
(That Viking Portable, all water-spotted and yellow—

Remember?) Or does mere distance lend a value
To things?—false, it may be, but the view is hardly cheapened.
Why this is, I'll never be able to tell you.

The smoke, those tiny cars, the whole urban milieu—
One can like *any*thing diminishment has sharpened.
Our painter friend, Lang, might show the whole thing yellow

And not be much off. It's nuance that counts, not color—
As in some late James novel, saved up for the long weekend,
And vivid with all the Master simply won't tell you.

How frail our generation has got, how sallow
And pinched with just surviving! We all go off the deep end
Finally, gold beaten thinly out to yellow.
And why this is, I'll never be able to tell you.

In Memory of the Unknown Poet, Robert Boardman Vaughn

> *But the essential advantage for a poet is not, to*
> *have a beautiful world with which to deal: it is to*
> *be able to see beneath both beauty and ugliness;*
> *to see the boredom, and the horror, and the glory.*
> —T. S. ELIOT

It was his story. It would always be his story.
It followed him; it overtook him finally—
The boredom, and the horror, and the glory.

Probably at the end he was not yet sorry,
Even as the boots were brutalizing him in the alley.
It was his story. It would always be his story,

Blown on a blue horn, full of sound and fury,
But signifying, O signifying magnificently
The boredom, and the horror, and the glory.

I picture the snow as falling without hurry
To cover the cobbles and the toppled ashcans completely.
It was his story. It would always be his story.

Lately he had wandered between St. Mark's Place and the Bowery,
Already half a spirit, mumbling and muttering sadly.
O the boredom, and the horror, and the glory!

All done now. But I remember the fiery
Hypnotic eye and the raised voice blazing with poetry.
It was his story and would always be his story—
The boredom, and the horror, and the glory.

Hell

"After so many years of pursuing the ideal,
I came home. But I had caught sight of it.
You see it sometimes in the blue-silver wake
Of island schooners, bound for Anegada, say.
And it takes other forms. I saw it flickering once
In torches by the railroad tracks in Medellín.

"When I was very young I thought that love would come
And seize and take me south and I would see the rose,
And that all ambiguities we knew would merge
Like orchids on a word. Say this:
I sought the immortal word."
                     So saying he went on
To join those who preceded him.
                     And there were those that followed.

Portrait with One Eye

They robbed you of your ticket
To the revolution, oh,
And then they stomped you good.
But nothing stops you.

You have identified yourself
To the police as quote
Lyric poet. What else?—
With fractured jaw. Orpheus,

Imperishable liar!
Your life's a poem still,
Broken iambs and all,
Jazz, jails—the complete works.

And one blue-silver line
Beyond the Antilles,
Vanishing . . . All fragments.
You who could scream across

The square in Cuernavaca,
At a friend you hadn't seen
For years, the one word, *bitch*,
And turn away—that's style!

Or this, your other voice,
This whisper along the wires
At night, like a dry wind,
Like conscience, always collect.

for Robert Boardman Vaughn

Portrait with Flashlight

What lonely aisles you prowled
In search of the forbidden,
Blinking your usher's torch,
Firefly of the balconies!

And when you found it—love!—
It was to pure French horns
Soaring above the plains
Of Saturday's Westerns.

The defiant eyes laughing
Into the sudden beam,
The soft Mexican curses,
The stains, the crushed corsages . . .

Off, off with those bright buttons,
Poor spy. Your heart's as dark
As theirs was and it speaks
With the same broken accent.

Those flowers, they blossom
Again now, tender buds
Of migraine—souvenirs.
And you call them poems,

Poems with hair slicked back,
Smelling of bay rum, sweat,
And hot buttered popcorn.
Furtive illuminations . . .

for Henri Coulette

Sonatina in Green

One spits on the sublime.
One lies in bed alone, reading
Yesterday's newspaper. One
Has composed a beginning, say,
A phrase or two. No more!
There has been traffic enough
In the boudoir of the muse.

And still they come, demanding entrance,
Noisy, and with ecstatic cries
Catching the perfume, forcing their way—
For them, what music? Only,
Distantly, through some door ajar,
Echoes, broken strains; and the garland
Crushed at the threshold.

        And we,
We few with the old instruments,
Obstinate, sounding the one string—
For us, what music? Only, at times,
The sunlight of late afternoon
That plays in the corner of a room,
Playing upon worn keys. At times,
Smells of decaying greenery, faint bouquets—
More than enough.

        And our cries
Diminish behind us:
        Cover
The bird cages! No more
Bargain days in the flower stalls!
There has been traffic enough
In the boudoir of the muse,
More than enough traffic. Or say
That one composed, in the end,
Another beginning, in spite of all this,
Sublime. Enough!

Closed are the grand boulevards,
And closed those mouths that made the lesser songs,
And the curtains drawn in the boudoir.

for my students

Sonatina in Yellow

Du schnell vergehendes Daguerreotyp
in meinen langsamer vergehenden Händen.
—RILKE

The pages of the album,
As they are turned, turn yellow; a word,
Once spoken, obsolete,
No longer what was meant. Say it.
The meanings come, or come back later,
Unobtrusive, taking their places.

Think of the past. Think of forgetting the past.
It was an exercise requiring further practice;
A difficult exercise, played through by someone else.
Overheard from another room, now,
It seems full of mistakes.
                              So the voice of your father,
Rising as from the next room still
With all the remote but true affection of the dead,
Repeats itself, insists,
Insisting you must listen, rises
In the familiar pattern of reproof
For some childish error, a nap disturbed,
Or vase, broken or overturned;
Rises and subsides. And you do listen.
Listen and forget. Practice forgetting.

Forgotten sunlight still
Blinds the eyes of faces in the album.
The faces fade, and there is only
A sort of meaning that comes back,
Or for the first time comes, but comes too late
To take the places of the faces.

                              Remember
The dead air of summer. Remember
The trees drawn up to their full height like fathers,
The underworld of shade you entered at their feet.

Enter the next room. Enter it quietly now,
Not to disturb your father sleeping there. *He stirs.*
Notice his clothes, how scrupulously clean,
Unwrinkled from the nap; his face, freckled with work,
Smoothed by a passing dream. The vase
Is not yet broken, the still young roses
Drink there from perpetual waters. *He rises, speaks . . .*

Repeat it now, no one was listening.
So your hand moves, moving across the keys,
And slowly the keys grow darker to the touch.

On the Death of Friends in Childhood

We shall not ever meet them bearded in heaven,
Nor sunning themselves among the bald of hell;
If anywhere, in the deserted schoolyard at twilight,
Forming a ring, perhaps, or joining hands
In games whose very names we have forgotten.
Come, memory, let us seek them there in the shadows.

Psalm and Lament

Hialeah, Florida

The clocks are sorry, the clocks are very sad.
One stops, one goes on striking the wrong hours.

And the grass burns terribly in the sun,
The grass turns yellow secretly at the roots.

Now suddenly the yard chairs look empty, the sky looks empty,
The sky looks vast and empty.

Out on Red Road the traffic continues; everything continues.
Nor does memory sleep; it goes on.

Out spring the butterflies of recollection,
And I think that for the first time I understand

The beautiful ordinary light of this patio
And even perhaps the dark rich earth of a heart.

(The bedclothes, they say, had been pulled down.
I will not describe it. I do not want to describe it.

No, but the sheets were drenched and twisted.
They were the very handkerchiefs of grief.)

Let summer come now with its schoolboy trumpets and fountains.
But the years are gone, the years are finally over.

And there is only
This long desolation of flower-bordered sidewalks

That runs to the corner, turns, and goes on,
That disappears and goes on

Into the black oblivion of a neighborhood and a world
Without billboards or yesterdays.

Sometimes a sad moon comes and waters the roof tiles.
But the years are gone. There are no more years.

in memory of my mother (1897–1974)

The Suicides

If we recall your voices
As softer now, it's only
That they must have drifted back

A long way to have reached us
Here, and upon such a wind
As crosses the high passes.

Nor does the blue of your eyes
(Remembered) cast much light on
The page ripped from the tablet.

―――――

Once there in the labyrinth,
You were safe from your reasons.
We stand, now, at the threshold,

Peering in, but the passage,
For us, remains obscure; the
Corridors are still bloody.

―――――

What you meant to prove you have
Proved—we did not care for you
Nearly enough. Meanwhile the

Bay was preparing herself
To receive you, the for once
Wholly adequate female

To your dark inclinations;
Under your care the pistol
Was slowly learning to flower

In the desired explosion,
Disturbing the careful part
And the briefly recovered

Fixed smile of a forgotten
Triumph; deep within the black
Forest of childhood that tree

Was already rising which,
With the length of your body,
Would cast the double shadow.

———

The masks by which we knew you
Have been torn from you. Even
Those mirrors, to which always

You must have turned to confide,
Cannot have recognized you,
Stripped, as you were, finally.

At the end of your shadow
There sat another, waiting,
Whose back was always to us.

———

When the last door had been closed,
You watched, inwardly raging,
For the first glimpse of your selves
Approaching, jangling their keys.

Musicians of the black keys,
At last you compose yourselves.
We hear the music raging
Under the lids we have closed.

in memory of J. and G. and J.

Incident in a Rose Garden

GARDENER

Sir, I encountered Death
Just now among our roses.
Thin as a scythe he stood there.

I knew him by his pictures.
He had his black coat on,
Black gloves, a broad black hat.

I think he would have spoken,
Seeing his mouth stood open.
Big it was, with white teeth.

As soon as he beckoned, I ran.
I ran until I found you.
Sir, I am quitting my job.

I want to see my sons
Once more before I die.
I want to see California.

MASTER

Sir, you must be that stranger
Who threatened my gardener.
This is my property, sir.

I welcome only friends here.

DEATH

Sir, I knew your father.
And we were friends at the end.

As for your gardener,
I did not threaten him.
Old men mistake my gestures.

I only meant to ask him
To show me to his master.
I take it you are he?

for Mark Strand

The Tourist from Syracuse

One of those men who can be a car salesman
or a tourist from Syracuse or a hired assassin.
—JOHN D. MACDONALD

You would not recognize me.
Mine is the face which blooms in
The dank mirrors of washrooms
As you grope for the light switch.

My eyes have the expression
Of the cold eyes of statues
Watching their pigeons return
From the feed you have scattered,

And I stand on my corner
With the same marble patience.
If I move at all, it is
At the same pace precisely

As the shade of the awning
Under which I stand waiting
And with whose blackness it seems
I am already blended.

I speak seldom, and always
In a murmur as quiet
As that of crowds which surround
The victims of accidents.

Shall I confess who I am?
My name is all names and none.
I am the used-car salesman,
The tourist from Syracuse,

The hired assassin, waiting.
I will stand here forever

Like one who has missed his bus—
Familiar, anonymous—

On my usual corner,
The corner at which you turn
To approach that place where now
You must not hope to arrive.

Fragment: To a Mirror

Behind that bland facade of yours,
What drafts are moving down what intricate maze
Of halls? What solitude of attics waits,
Bleak, at the top of the still-hidden stair?
And are those windows yours that open out
On such spectacular views?
The parks nearby,
Whose statues doze forever in the sun?
Those stricken avenues,
Along which great palms wither and droop down
Their royal fronds,
And the parade is drummed
To a sudden, inexplicable halt?
                              Tell me,
Is this the promised absence I foresee
In you, that time when no breath any more
Shall stir the surface of the sleeping pond,
And you shall have back your rest at last,
Your half of nothingness?

At a Rehearsal of "Uncle Vanya"

NURSE: *The crows might get them.*

You mean well, Doctor,
But are—forgive me—
A bit of a crank,

A friend they may love
But cannot listen
To long, for yawning.

When you are gone, though,
They move up close to
The stove's great belly.

Yes, they are burning
Your forests, Doctor,
The dark green forests.

There is a silence
That falls between them
Like snow, like deep snow.

Horses have gone lame
Crossing the waste lands
Between two people.

Doctor, who is well?
Leaning out across
Our own distances,

We hear the old nurse
Calling her chickens
In now: *chook chook chook.*

It's cold in Russia.
We sit here, Doctor,
In the crows' shadow.

In the Greenroom

How reassuring
To discover them
In the greenroom. Here,

Relaxing, they drop
The patronymics
By which we had come

To know them. The cross
Are no longer cross,
The old dance, nor have

The young sacrificed
Their advantages.
In this it is like

A kind of heaven
They rise to simply
By being themselves.

The sound of the axe
Biting the wood is
Rewound on the tape.

What is this green for
If not renewal?

Last Days of Prospero

The aging magician retired to his island.
It was not so green as he remembered,
Nor did the sea caress its headlands
With the customary nuptial music.

He did not mind. He would not mind,
So long as the causeway to the mainland
Were not repaired, so long as the gay
Little tourist steamer never again

Lurched late into harbor, and no one
Applied for a license to reopen
The shuttered, gilt casino. Better,
He thought, an isle unvisited

Except for the sea birds come to roost
On the roofs of the thousand ruined cabañas,
Survivors; or the strayed whale, offshore,
Suspicious, surfacing to spout,

Noble as any fountain of Mílan . . .
The cave? That was as he had left it,
Amply provisioned against the days
To come. His cloak? Neat on its hanger;

The painted constellations, though faded
With damp a little, still glittered
And seemed in the dark to move on course.
His books? He knew where they were drowned.

(What tempests he had caused, what lightnings
Loosed in the rigging of the world!)
If now it was all to do again,
Nothing was lacking to his purpose.

Some change in the wording of the charm,
Some slight reshuffling of negative

And verb, perhaps: that should suffice.
So, so. Meanwhile he paced the strand,

Debating, as old men will, with himself
Or the waves, though, as it was, the sea
Seemed only to go on washing and washing
Itself, as if to be clean of something.

On a Painting by Patient B of the
Independence State Hospital for the Insane

1

These seven houses have learned to face one another,
But not at the expected angles. Those silly brown lumps,
That are probably meant for hills and not other houses,
After ages of being themselves, though naturally slow,
Are learning to be exclusive without offending.
The arches and entrances (down to the right out of sight)
Have mastered the lesson of remaining closed.
And even the skies keep a certain understandable distance,
For these are the houses of the very rich.

2

One sees their children playing with leopards, tamed
At great cost, or perhaps it is only other children,
For none of these objects is anything more than a spot,
And perhaps there are not any children but only leopards
Playing with leopards, and perhaps there are only the spots.
And the little maids that hang from the windows like tongues,
Calling the children in, admiring the leopards,
Are the dashes a child might represent motion by means of,
Or dazzlement possibly, the brilliance of solid-gold houses.

3

The clouds resemble those empty balloons in cartoons
Which approximate silence. These clouds, if clouds they are
('And not the smoke from the seven aspiring chimneys),
The more one studies them the more it appears
They too have expressions. One might almost say
They have their habits, their wrong opinions, that their
Impassivity masks an essentially lovable foolishness,
And they will be given names by those who live under them
Not public like mountains' but private like companions'.

76

Counting the Mad

This one was put in a jacket,
This one was sent home,
This one was given bread and meat
But would eat none,
And this one cried No No No No
All day long.

This one looked at the window
As though it were a wall,
This one saw things that were not there,
This one things that were,
And this one cried No No No No
All day long.

This one thought himself a bird,
This one a dog,
And this one thought himself a man,
An ordinary man,
And cried and cried No No No No
All day long.

Bus Stop

Lights are burning
In quiet rooms
Where lives go on
Resembling ours.

The quiet lives
That follow us—
These lives we lead
But do not own—

Stand in the rain
So quietly
When we are gone,
So quietly . . .

And the last bus
Comes letting dark
Umbrellas out—
Black flowers, black flowers.

And lives go on.
And lives go on
Like sudden lights
At street corners

Or like the lights
In quiet rooms
Left on for hours,
Burning, burning.

October: A Song

Summer, goodbye.
The days grow shorter.
Cranes walk the fairway now
In careless order.

They step so gradually
Toward the distant green
They might almost be brushstrokes
Animating a screen.

Mists canopy
The water hazard.
Nearby, a little flag
Lifts, brave but frazzled.

Under sad clouds
Two white-capped golfers
Stand looking off, dreamy and strange,
Like young girls in Balthus.

Another Song

Merry the green, the green hill shall be merry.
Hungry, the owlet shall seek out the mouse,
And Jack his Joan, but they shall never marry.

And snows shall fly, the big flakes fat and furry.
Lonely, the traveler shall seek out the house,
And Jack his Joan, but they shall never marry.

Weary the soldiers go, and come back weary,
Up a green hill and down the withered hill,
And Jack from Joan, and they shall never marry.

The Sometime Dancer Blues

When the lights go on uptown,
Why do you feel so low, honey,
Why do you feel so low-down?

When the piano and the trombone start,
Why do you feel so blue, honey,
Like a rubber glove had reached in for your heart?

O when the dancers take the floor,
Why don't you step on out, honey,
Why won't you step out with them anymore?

The stars are gone and the night is dark,
Except for the radium, honey,
That glows on the hands of the bedside clock,

The little hands that go around and around,
O as silently as time, honey,
Without a sound, without a sound.

Little Elegy

Weep, all you girls
Who prize good looks and song.
Mack, the canary, is dead.

A girl very much like you
Kept him by her twelve months
Close as a little brother.

He perched where he pleased,
Hopped, chirping, from breast to breast,
And fed, sometimes, pecking from her mouth.

O lucky bird! But death
Plucks from the air even
The swiftest, the most favored.

Red are the eyes of his mistress now.
On us, her remaining admirers,
They do not yet quite focus.

after Catullus

Sea-Wind: A Song

Sea-wind, you rise
From the night waves below,
Not that we see you come and go,
But as the blind know things we know
And feel you on our face,
And all you are
Or ever were is space,
Sea-wind, come from so far,
To fill us with this restlessness
That will outlast your own—
So the fig tree,
When you are gone,
Sea-wind, still bends and leans out toward the sea
And goes on blossoming alone.

after Rilke

Last Evening: At the Piano

And night and far to go—
For hours the convoys had rolled by
Like storm clouds in a troubled sky;
    He'd gone on playing, though,

And raised his eyes to hers,
Which had become his mirror now,
So filled were they with his clenched brow,
    And the pain to come, or worse;

And then the image blurred.
She stood at the window in the gloom
And looked back through the fading room—
    Outside, a fresh wind stirred—

And noticed across a chair
The officer's jacket he had flung
There earlier; and now it hung
    Like the coats scarecrows wear

And the bird-shadows flee and scatter from;
Or like the skin of some great battle-drum.

after Rilke

The Metamorphoses of a Vampire

The woman, meanwhile, from her strawberry mouth—
Twisting and turning like a snake on coals,
And kneading her breasts against her corset-stays—
Let flow these words, all interfused with musk:
"My lips are moist; and I know how to make
A man forget all conscience deep in bed.
I dry all tears on my triumphant breasts
And set old men to laughing like young boys.
For those who see me naked and unveiled,
I take the place of sun, and moon, and stars!
I am, dear scholar, so well schooled in pleasure
That when I smother a man in my smooth arms
Or when I abandon to his teeth my bosom—
Shy and voluptuous, tender and robust—
Upon these cushions groaning with delight,
The impotent angels would damn themselves for me!"

When she had sucked the marrow from my bones,
And, languidly, I turned toward her intending
A love-kiss in return, I saw there only
A sort of leathery wineskin filled with pus!
I shut my eyes in a cold fright, and when
I opened them again to the good day,
Beside me lay no mannequin whose power
Seemed to have come from drinking human blood:
There trembled a confusion of old bones
Which creaked in turning like a weathervane,
Or like a signboard on an iron pole
Swung by the wind through the long winter nights.

translated from Baudelaire

Young Girls Growing Up (1911)

No longer do they part and scatter so hopelessly before you,
But they will stop and put an elbow casually
On the piano top and look quite frankly at you;
Their pale reflections glide there then like swans.

What you say to them now is not lost. They listen to the end
And—little heart-shaped chins uplifted—seem
Just on the point of breaking into song;
Nor is a short conversation more than they can stand.

When they turn away they do so slowly, and mean no harm;
And it seems their backs are suddenly broader also.
You picture yourself in the avenue below, masked by trees,
And, just as the streetlamps go on, you glance up:

There, there at the window, blotting out the light. . . !
Weeks pass and perhaps you meet unexpectedly.
Now they come forward mournfully, hands outstretched,
Asking why you are such a stranger, what has changed?

But when you seek them out, they only
Crouch in a window seat and pretend to read,
And have no look to spare you, and seem cruel.
And this is why there are men who wander aimlessly through
    cities!

This is why there are cities and darkness and a river,
And men who stride along the embankment now, without a plan,
And turn their collars up against the moon,
Saying to one another, *Live, we must try to live, my friend!*

after Kafka

Variations on a Text by Vallejo

Me moriré en Paris con aguacero. . . .

I will die in Miami in the sun,
On a day when the sun is very bright,
A day like the days I remember, a day like other days,
A day that nobody knows or remembers yet,
And the sun will be bright then on the dark glasses of strangers
And in the eyes of a few friends from my childhood
And of the surviving cousins by the graveside,
While the diggers, standing apart, in the still shade of the palms,
Rest on their shovels, and smoke,
Speaking in Spanish softly, out of respect.

I think it will be on a Sunday like today,
Except that the sun will be out, the rain will have stopped,
And the wind that today made all the little shrubs kneel down;
And I think it will be a Sunday because today,
When I took out this paper and began to write,
Never before had anything looked so blank,
My life, these words, the paper, the gray Sunday;
And my dog, quivering under a table because of the storm,
Looked up at me, not understanding,
And my son read on without speaking, and my wife slept.

Donald Justice is dead. One Sunday the sun came out,
It shone on the bay, it shone on the white buildings,
The cars moved down the street slowly as always, so many,
Some with their headlights on in spite of the sun,
And after a while the diggers with their shovels
Walked back to the graveside through the sunlight,
And one of them put his blade into the earth
To lift a few clods of dirt, the black marl of Miami,
And scattered the dirt, and spat,
Turning away abruptly, out of respect.

Homage to the Memory of
Wallace Stevens

1

Hartford is cold today but no colder for your absence.
The rain is green over Avon and, since your death, the sky
Has been blue many times with a blue you did not imagine.

The judges of Key West sit soberly in black
But only because it is their accustomed garb,
And the sea sings with the same voice still, neither serious
     nor sorry.

The walls past which you walked in your white suit,
Ponderous, pondering French pictures,
Are no less vivid now. Not one is turned to the wall.

The actuarial tables are not upset.
The mail travels back and forth to Ceylon as before.
The gold leaf peels in season and is renewed.

And there are heroes who falter but do not fall,
Or fall without faltering and without fault,
But you were not one of them. Nevertheless,

The poet practicing his scales
Thinks of you as his thumbs slip clumsily under and under,
Avoiding the darker notes.

2

The *the* has become an *a*. The dictionary
Closed at dusk, along with the zoo in the park.

And the wings of the swans are folded now like the sheets of a long
     letter.
Who borrows your French words and postures now?

3

The opera of the gods is finished,
And the applause is dying.
The chorus will soon be coming down from the clouds.
Even their silence may be understood
As a final platitude of sorts, a summing up.

The tireless dancers have retired at last
To a small apartment on a treeless street.
But, oh, the pas de deux of Eden begins again
On cot-springs creaking like the sun and moon!
The operation of the universe is temporarily suspended.

What has been good? What has been beautiful?
The tuning up, or the being put away?
The instruments have nothing more to say.
Now they will sleep on plush and velvet till
Our breath revives them to new flutterings, new adieux—

And to the picnic all the singers come,
Minus their golden costumes, but no less gods for that.
Now all quotations from the text apply,
Including the laughter, including the offstage thunder,
Including even this almost human cry.

Hartford, 1969

After a Phrase Abandoned
by Wallace Stevens

The alp at the end of the street
—STEVENS' NOTEBOOKS

The alp at the end of the street
Occurs in the dreams of the town.
Over burgher and shopkeeper,
Massive, he broods,
A snowy-headed father
Upon whose knees his children
No longer climb;
Or is reflected
In the cool, unruffled lakes of
Their minds, at evening,
After their day in the shops,
As shadow only, shapeless
As a wind that has stopped blowing.

Grandeur, it seems,
Comes down to this in the end—
A street of shops
With white shutters
Open for business . . .

Landscape with Little Figures

There once were some pines, a canal, a piece of sky.
The pines are the houses now of the very poor,
Huddled together, in a blue, ragged wind.
Children go whistling their dogs, down by the mudflats,
Once the canal. There's a red ball lost in the weeds.
It's winter, it's after supper, it's goodbye.
O goodbye to the houses, the children, the little red ball,
And the pieces of sky that will go on falling for days.

In Bertram's Garden

Jane looks down at her organdy skirt
As if *it* somehow were the thing disgraced,
For being there, on the floor, in the dirt,
And she catches it up about her waist,
Smooths it out along one hip,
And pulls it over the crumpled slip.

On the porch, green-shuttered, cool,
Asleep is Bertram, that bronze boy,
Who, having wound her around a spool,
Sends her spinning like a toy
Out to the garden, all alone,
To sit and weep on a bench of stone.

Soon the purple dark will bruise
Lily and bleeding heart and rose,
And the little Cupid lose
Eyes and ears and chin and nose,
And Jane lie down with others soon
Naked to the naked moon.

Heart

Heart, let us this once reason together.
Thou art a child no longer. Only think
What sport the neighbors have from us, not without cause.
These nightly sulks, these clamorous demonstrations!
Already they tell of thee a famous story.
An antique, balding spectacle such as thou art,
Affecting still that childish, engaging stammer
With all the seedy innocence of an overripe pomegranate!
Henceforth, let us conduct ourselves more becomingly!

And still I hear thee, beating thy little fist
Against the walls. My dear, have I not led thee,
Dawn after streaky dawn, besotted, home?
And still these threats to have off as before?
From thee, who wouldst lose thyself in the next street?
Go then, O my inseparable, this once more.
Afterwards we will take thought for our good name.

Men at Forty

Men at forty
Learn to close softly
The doors to rooms they will not be
Coming back to.

At rest on a stair landing,
They feel it moving
Beneath them now like the deck of a ship,
Though the swell is gentle.

And deep in mirrors
They rediscover
The face of the boy as he practices tying
His father's tie there in secret

And the face of that father,
Still warm with the mystery of lather.
They are more fathers than sons themselves now.
Something is filling them, something

That is like the twilight sound
Of the crickets, immense,
Filling the woods at the foot of the slope
Behind their mortgaged houses.

The Thin Man

I indulge myself
In rich refusals.
Nothing suffices.

I hone myself to
This edge. Asleep, I
Am a horizon.

Dreams of Water

1

An odd silence
Falls as we enter
The cozy ship's-bar.

The captain, smiling,
Unfolds his spyglass
And offers to show you

The obscene shapes
Of certain islands,
Low in the offing.

I sit by in silence.

2

People in raincoats
Stand looking out from
Ends of piers.

A fog gathers;
And little tugs,
Growing uncertain

Of their position,
Start to complain
With the deep and bearded

Voices of fathers.

3

The season is ending.
White verandas
Curve away.

The hotel seems empty
But, once inside,
I hear a great splashing.

Behind doors
Grandfathers loll
In steaming tubs,

Huge, unblushing.

To Satan in Heaven

Forgive, Satan, virtue's pedants, all such
As have broken our habits, or had none,
The keepers of promises, prize-winners,
Meek as leaves in the wind's circus, evenings;
Our simple wish to be elsewhere forgive
Shy touchers of library atlases,
Envious of bird-flight, the whale's submersion;
And us forgive who have forgotten how,
The melancholy, who, lacing a shoe,
Choose not to continue, the merely bored,
Who have modeled our lives after cloud-shapes;
For which confessing, have mercy on us,
The different and the indifferent,
In inverse proportion to our merit,
For we have affirmed thee secretly, by
Candle-glint in the polish of silver,
Between courses, murmured amenities,
Seen thee in mirrors by morning, shaving,
Or head in loose curls on the next pillow,
Reduced thee to our own scope and purpose,
Satan, who, though in heaven, downward yearned,
As the butterfly, weary of flowers,
Longs for the cocoon or the looping net.

Poem

This poem is not addressed to you.
You may come into it briefly,
But no one will find you here, no one.
You will have changed before the poem will.

Even while you sit there, unmovable,
You have begun to vanish. And it does not matter.
The poem will go on without you.
It has the spurious glamor of certain voids.

It is not sad, really, only empty.
Once perhaps it was sad, no one knows why.
It prefers to remember nothing.
Nostalgias were peeled from it long ago.

Your type of beauty has no place here.
Night is the sky over this poem.
It is too black for stars.
And do not look for any illumination.

You neither can nor should understand what it means.
Listen, it comes without guitar,
Neither in rags nor any purple fashion.
And there is nothing in it to comfort you.

Close your eyes, yawn. It will be over soon.
You will forget the poem, but not before
It has forgotten you. And it does not matter.
It has been most beautiful in its erasures.

O bleached mirrors! Oceans of the drowned!
Nor is one silence equal to another.
And it does not matter what you think.
This poem is not addressed to you.

The Piano Teachers: A Memoir
of the Thirties

1. *It Was a Kind and Northern Face: Mrs. Snow*

Busts of the great composers
Glimmered in niches, pale stars . . .
                              Poor Mrs. Snow!
She used to tower above us like an alp,
An avalanche threatening sudden
Unasked for kindnesses.
                              Exiled, alone,
She did not quite complain,
But only sighed and looked off elsewhere,
Regretting the Symphony, perhaps.
                              In dreams, though,
The new palms of the yard,
The one brilliant flame tree
Must have changed back into the elms and maples
Of old, decaying streets.
—Sometimes the inadequate floor quaked
With the effort of her rising.
The great legs, swollen and empurpled,
Could hardly support the hugeness
Of her need.
                              And if
They did not understand—her friends—
She had, in any case, the artistic
Temperament,
                              which isolates—
And saves!
                              Dust motes
Among the Chinese jars. Etchings
Of Greece and Rome. The photograph
Of Mrs. Eddy.
                              Brown sky, so old,
Fading above us all.

2. *Busted Dreams: Mrs. L.*

The faint odour of your patchouli. . . .

The mother's gypsy skirt
Flared like the daughter's.
                    Together
They demonstrated the foxtrot,
Gliding across the living room
And back, each time avoiding
With the same heartbreaking little swoop
                              or dip
The shabby, cloth-draped, pushed-back, suddenly looming
Sofa.
              On the piano top,
A nest of souvenirs:
                    paper
Flowers, old programs, a broken fan,
Like a bird's broken wing.
—And sometimes Mr. L. himself
Came back, recurring, like a dream.
He would have brought real flowers.
                    Thin,
Demanding, his voice soared after dark
In the old opera between them.
But no one saw the blows, only
An occasional powdered bruise,
Genteel. Did he come all the way from
Cuba each time for this?
              The children
Were loosed upon the neighborhood
To wander. In the summer-idle
School yard they were the last ghosts
Of the swings.
                    Nine o'clock, ten o'clock.
A thousand reconcilings.
                    The moon . . .

Next day,
On the Havana ferryboat again,
A little, overneat man at the rail,
Examining the waves, his nails.
And she,
Plunging the stiff comb suddenly deep
Into her hair, would be just turning
To greet some half-forgotten pupil at the door.

3. *Those Tropic Afternoons: Mrs. K.*

But in Miami?

Four or five o'clock.
        Late summer
Around us like a cocoon,
Gauzy and intimate.
—And sometimes she succumbed
To the passion of a nocturne,
The fury of the climax
Ascending through the folds
Of secret and abandoned flesh
Into those bitten finger-ends
That pressed from the unsuspecting keys
A certain exaltation—
Only to die away at last
Into a long fermata.

(Satisfaction. The brief
And inward smile.)

        Meanwhile,
Dappled with shade of tangelo and mango,
In canvas deck chair that sagged, the husband
Sat peering out across
A forlorn sea of half-mown lawn,
Balding, out of work, a sad
Columbus.
        The drone
Of traffic, far off, seemed
To reassure: 54th Street
Still led off toward the Glades at sunset.

        And the child—
What had I to be afraid of?
My yellow lesson book

Open on the rack
To that blue, cloudy look of hers.
     The fan,
Placed on the floor, clicked
With every turn—metronome
Of boredom.
     Once more, dear: Larghetto.
     Laborers
Coming home, the long day ending.

Mrs. Snow

Busts of the great composers glimmered in niches,
Pale stars. Poor Mrs. Snow, who could forget her,
Counting the time out in that hushed falsetto?
(How early we begin to grasp what kitsch is!)
But when she loomed above us like an alp,
We little towns below could feel her shadow.
Somehow her nods of approval seemed to matter
More than the stray flakes drifting from her scalp.
Her etchings of ruins, her mass-production Mings
Were our first culture: she put us in awe of things.
And once, with her help, I composed a waltz,
Too innocent to be completely false,
Perhaps, but full of marvellous clichés.
She beamed and softened then.
                                   Ah, those were the days.

The Pupil

Picture me, the shy pupil at the door,
One small, tight fist clutching the dread Czerny.
Back then time was still harmony, not money,
And I could spend a whole week practicing for
That moment on the threshold.
                              Then to take courage,
And enter, and pass among mysterious scents,
And sit quite straight, and with a frail confidence
Assault the keyboard with a childish flourish!

Only to lose my place, or forget the key,
And almost doubt the very metronome
(Outside, the traffic, the laborers going home),
And still to bear on across Chopin or Brahms,
Stupid and wild with love equally for the storms
Of C# minor and the calms of C.

On a Woman of Spirit Who Taught
Both Piano and Dance

Thanks to the Powers-
That-Used-To-Be for all her rouges
And powders, those small cosmetic subterfuges
Which were the gloss upon her book of hours;
And to Madam L. herself, whose heart
Was a hummingbird's, and flew from art to art.

Dance Lessons of the Thirties

Wafts of old incense mixed with Cuban coffee
Hung on the air; a fan turned; it was summer.
And (of the buried life) some last aroma
Still clung to the tumbled cushions of the sofa.

At lesson time, pushed back, it used to be
The thing we managed somehow just to miss
With our last-second dips and twirls—all this
While the Victrola wound down gradually.

And this was their exile, those brave ladies who taught us
So much of art, and stepped off to their doom
Demonstrating the foxtrot with their daughters
Endlessly around some sad and makeshift ballroom.

O little lost Bohemias of the suburbs!

After-school Practice: A Short Story

Rain that masks the world
Presses it back too hard against
His forehead at the pane.
Three stories down, umbrellas
Are borne along the current of the sidewalk; a bus
Glides like a giant planchette
In some mysterious pattern through the traffic.
Alone now, he feels lost in the new apartment;
He feels some dark cloud shouldering in.
His wish, if he could have one,
Would be for the baby next door to cry out
This minute, signifying end of nap.
Then he could practice. (Apartment life
Is full of these considerations.)
But when finally this does happen,
He still for a time postpones the first chord.
He looks around, full of secrets;
His strange deep thoughts have brought, so far, no harm.
Carefully, with fists and elbows, he prepares
One dark, tremendous chord
Never heard before—his own thunder!
And strikes.
            And the strings will quiver with it
A long time before the held pedal
Gives up the sound completely—this throbbing
Of the piano's great exposed heart.
Then, soberly, he begins his scales.

And gradually the storm outside dies away also.

The Sunset Maker

The speaker is a friend of the dead composer,
Eugene Bestor. He is seated on the terrace of
his townhouse, from which there is a view of
the Gulf of Mexico.

The Bestor papers have come down to me.
I would imagine, though, they're destined for
The quiet archival twilight of some library.
Meanwhile, I have been sorting scores. The piece
I linger over sometimes is the last,
The "Elegy." So many black, small notes!
They fly above the staff like flags of mourning;
And I can hear the sounds the notes intend.
(Some duo of the mind produces them,
Without error, ghost-music materializing;
Faintly, of course, like whispers overheard.)
And then? I might work up the piano part,
If it mattered. But where is there a cellist
This side of the causeway? And who plays Bestor now?

This time of day I listen to the surf
Myself; I listen to it from my terrace.
The sun eases its way down through the palms,
Scattering colors—a bit of orange, some blues.
Do you know that painting of Bonnard's, *The Terrace?*
It shows a water pitcher blossom-ready
And a woman who bends down to the doomed blossoms—
One of the fates, in orange—and then the sea
With its own streaks of orange, harmonious.
It used to hang in the Phillips near the Steinway.
But who could call back now the web of sound
The cello and the piano wove together
There in the Phillips not so long ago?
The three plucked final chords—someone might still
Recall, if not the chords, then the effect
They made—as if the air were troubled somehow.
As if—but everything there is is that.

Impressions shimmering; broken light. The world
Is French, if it is anything. Or was.
One phrase the cello had, an early phrase,
That does stay with me, mixed a little now
With Bonnard's colors. A brief rush upward, then
A brief subsiding. Can it be abstract?—
As Stravinsky said it must be to be music.
But what if a phrase *could* represent a thought—
Or feeling, should we say?—without existence
Apart from the score where someone catches it?

Inhale, exhale: a drawn-out gasp or sigh.
Falling asleep, I hear it. It is just there.
I don't say what it means. And I agree
It's sentimental to suppose my friend
Survives in just this fragment, this tone-row
A hundred people halfway heard one Sunday
And one of them no more than half remembers.
The hard early years of study, those still,
Sequestered mornings in the studio,
The perfect ear, the technique, the great gift
All have come down to this one ghostly phrase.
And soon nobody will recall the sound
Those six notes made once or that there were six.

Hear the gulls. That's our local music.
I like it myself; ánd, as you can see,
Our sunset maker studied with Bonnard.

MEMOIR

Piano Lessons: Notes on a
Provincial Culture

So now it is vain for the singer to burst into clamour
With the great black piano appassionata. The glamour
Of childish days is upon me. . . .

A P I A N O   L E S S O N in those days cost fifty cents and lasted for half an hour. At that price my parents, though far from well off, were able to afford a weekly lesson for me all through the Depression years. I sensed even then that the lessons represented an ambition for gentility on my mother's part. Mother had studied piano herself as a girl and would still play certain favorite hymns and old recital pieces with a noisy and cheerful confidence. In bourgeois life it is usually the mother to whom the child's first cultural or artistic stirrings and strivings can be traced, and this was certainly true in my life.

Sometimes the half hour allotted to a lesson would stretch out to an hour or more, if no other pupil was scheduled. Often, with Mrs. L. or Mrs. K., my last two teachers, none would be. It was clear to everyone, themselves included, that they were dedicated less to teaching than to the small sums their teaching brought in. This obvious fact embarrassed no one. Times were hard and these things were understood. Afternoons with them I remember now as always hot and summerlike, time going by at a slow pace, drawn out toward dusk like a long ritardando. This was in Miami, and even in the winter months the electric fan might be set on the floor beside us, where it turned with a click like a metronome's. Yellow Schirmer editions of Czerny and Chopin lay stacked on the closed lid of a baby grand, along with assorted sheet music, popular and classical. Fan turning, teacher close beside me, I would run through my scales, my exercises, week after week.

My first piano teacher, a Mrs. Snow, was more inspiring. Only last week, looking through one of my mother's albums, I came across a snapshot of Mrs. Snow. Under a corner of sky now brown and faded she stands with smiling pupil, unidentified, in front of a cottage above whose entrance a signboard spells out MUSICLAND. She wears a choker of beads and clutches a crushed handkerchief. I had forgotten her double chin. The snapshot is not in color—it is too ancient for that—but the color of the flowered chiffon dress she is wearing does all the same come back to me, a bleached-out coppery or rust tone. And now suddenly her very body odor, to which I must have grown accustomed as a child, comes back as well, intimate and powdery.

We had come together by the sort of chance that later seems like destiny. One Saturday night my mother and father and I were downtown shopping, as we often were, for the stores stayed open well into the evening then. Heading back to our parked car along busy Miami Avenue, mother and I made a last sweep through the Cromer-Cassell's department store. In the basement we came upon one of the rhythm bands which were a feature of that era, like Tom Thumb weddings and street-corner evangelists. This band was just finishing up a performance; it must have been near closing time. Eight or ten small children, all wearing overseas caps and blue-and-white shoulder-length capes, stood huddled together as they tapped and banged away at snare drums and wood blocks and triangles or shook their tambourines and castanets and tiny hand-bells, which were held up at ear level and jiggled. Mother and I paused to listen. The musicians stood in two rows on a low platform, struggling with the beat, following a sort of wand waved by the large fairy godmother of a woman who led them. This was Mrs. Snow. Mother took my hand in hers. I was not quite six years old, and I had never before that night seen a musical group of any kind outside of church.

My wish must have been obvious. Before long I had a snare drum and cape of my own. (The drum was my sixth-birthday present; the receipt for it is pasted in a scrapbook—Cromer-Cassell's, $6.50.) Soon the drum had given way to lessons on the piano, and none too soon for me. The sounds of the piano, with all their sonorities and relations, were like some favorite dessert to me after the pitchless, snarly note of the snare.

Mrs. Snow was not only leader of the band; she also gave piano lessons. The rhythm band was a sideline; at heart she was a serious musician. She had recently come south from Massachusetts. Her northern name calls back for me even now the whiteness of her hair and something also in her character that over the years was to remain remote and otherworldly, but she could be soft and melting too, motherly and enfolding to a child my age. How well the name suited her she realized, often commenting on it, with a little laugh. Snow itself was of course unknown to us in Miami, and even New Englanders were rare. Many people from the North had moved down for reasons of health to what we called the tropics; or so we assumed. Probably that was the case with Mrs. Snow herself, for she never looked truly well. I remember still the thick white hose she sometimes had to wear over her swollen and empurpled legs. She saw no doctors, being a Christian Scientist. To stand with swollen legs must have been painful, but to stand for long periods conducting a group of children with noisemakers could only have been torment. Stoic though she was, she allowed herself a high stool upon which she could lean or sit back, keeping time with her baton.

Mrs. Snow believed in method and exactness, even for a pupil just starting school, like me. Along with her older pupils, I was required to take down during the first part of each lesson a simple sort of musical dictation. Upon our music pads, which bore the Baconian motto "Writing makes the exact man," we would set down key signatures, notes, rests, scales, and, under guidance, a few harmonic progressions, chiefly cadences. Before long we were being encouraged to compose our own simple melodies, to be harmonized in consultation. Each week to our loose-leaf notebooks was added a page containing the picture of a famous composer, which resembled in style the small busts commanding the mantelpiece and shelves and sills of the Snow cottage. For Christmas that year—it was 1931— I received from my teacher a T. Presser card, sentimentally tinted: the face of the young Mozart superimposed upon a photograph of his "Geburtshaus." How foreign it all seemed! Somewhere beyond Miami lay faraway New England and, beyond that, Europe, and in Europe were Germany and Austria, which I could picture as on a map with the birthplaces of the great composers indicated by dots. There was just such a musical map in our notebooks.

Every Wednesday afternoon my mother would pick me up after school in the old Essex she had only recently learned to drive. I would open the lunch pail into which she had packed a sandwich and cookies for the expedition, though it was a drive of not more than four or five miles. All day in the first-grade classroom I would have been aware of what day it was and of what the afternoon held. By the time we were crossing the 17th Avenue bridge over the Miami

River the sense of adventure would be strong in me. (This was not far from where the Orange Bowl now stands, and at that time it was an especially picturesque residential area, with quantities of red and yellow crotons along the approaches to the bridge, and a scattering of traveler's palms, not to mention several small caves hidden in the rocks below.) It used to seem to me in those days that we were crossing a frontier into a different world.

My mother and I were soon members of a circle which, for all I know, may have included every child in the city taking music lessons, along with, of course, their mothers. There was a large and quite grand building in which musical galas and banquets took place. It may have been Miami High School, from which I would graduate a decade later, but if so, the thought never crossed my mind when I was attending classes there. In any case, there was then somewhere a great labyrinthine building, of unusual intricacy, just the sort of building which makes an ideal setting for dreams, with numerous arches and arcades and courtyards. I remember one performance in a courtyard in which I took part. It was a pantomime enacting the story of Jonah and the Whale, one of several numbers during the course of a musical evening. I was small enough to play Jonah, and a young man much larger than I played the Whale. I was to struggle free from our joint costume during the performance. What this had to do with music escapes me now.

The little I knew of social and class distinctions I must have learned from these affairs. The near poor, like us, mingled democratically with the wealthy few. The glamor of it for me came more from the newness and strangeness than from any hints of wealth or fame. One or two retired coloraturas, whose names grew familiar through repeated appearances as sponsors on a succession of printed programs, represented the sum total of the local famous, musically. In 1932, when Paderewski appeared in concert, it was at the enormous Methodist church downtown known as the White Temple; from one of its balconies my mother and I, like hundreds of others, gazed down at a small man foreshortened by distance. Now and then, invited to a recital, we did glimpse the sumptuous interior of some splendid house. And there were occasional holiday parties, usually outdoors, behind massive vine-covered mortared walls, under tall palms. We children were often got up in costume for these, like juveniles attached to a touring stage company. All these years I have kept an impression of sparkling perfect teeth flashed by the seven- and eight-year-old beauties of those houses. Once, on a raised outdoor terrace, upon a glass-topped table the like of which I had not before seen, appeared a plate of tiny blue sandwiches, cut into triangles. I wondered at once how *blue* would taste. No one seemed to be looking. I closed my fist loosely over one of the tiny sandwiches and made my way quickly down into the yard and around a corner to sample it in secret. It was delicious.

Our parents must have known—how could they have failed to know?—that nothing at all practical could come from any of this. The half-dollar each week was like a coin paid the gypsy for her improbable prophesyings. The giving and taking of such lessons goes on even now, I know, and probably for the same reasons as ever, but during the Depression there was a special desperation in it all. More than one of the little girls I knew, their mothers fallen under the spell of Shirley Temple, had their hair done in curls and studied tap dancing. Tap was the ballet of the poor, and at the end of a school day you could hear a confusion of shoetaps clattering off down the corridors of Allapattah Elementary. As for me, my Georgia aunts and uncles, during our summer round of visits, never failed to ask what I wanted to be when I grew up. I liked to have an answer ready—accountant, aviator, first-baseman—but such answers were polite fictions. Not for a long while yet would I want to be anything in particular. What I liked more than anything else was music, but I did not envision myself in the long tails and with the streaming hair of a Paderewski, taking bows. All the same, I see now that, with my first lesson, I had already begun to escape from the kind of life my parents knew.

After two or three years my lessons with Mrs. Snow came to an end. No more "March Militaire" at recitals for me, no more blue sandwiches. It may be that Mrs. Snow had become too old and frail to meet the demands she put on herself. Perhaps she died or went back to New England. I wish I knew; I think very kindly of her. She taught me the language of music, how to read and write it, and her training left me very quick at sight-reading, a knack that has enabled me all my life to read through much of the literature for piano, not without mistakes, but without hard work either, and with the pure, conscienceless pleasure of the amateur.

Or it may be that, for a year or two, my parents could not afford the cost of lessons. The family version is that breaking off the lessons was my idea. I know there were days when, instead of practicing, I would rather have been out-of-doors with the other boys, playing ball. Music had come to seem a soft and feminine world to me, and the practice hour was *very* solitary. I can remember moments of impatience, the faint squeaking of the piano stool as it twisted in restless quarter-turns beneath me, and all the while the voices of friends at play in the vacant lot directly across from our house. But I wonder now if stopping the lessons may not have had something to do with the death of my best friend, a boy from down the street as skinny and full of nerves as I was, who lingered on for months before his rheumatic fever finally killed him. His death terrified us that late spring when I was nine, all of us about his age who, dressed at our neatest, acted as pallbearers one sad afternoon. I was to weep off and on all summer, grievously. At some point during that period, I know, I was no longer taking piano lessons; that is all I can say for sure now. Before the summer was out I had fallen ill myself, with osteomyelitis, and during the long recuperation, which lasted through the winter and most of the next spring, there was no question of resuming lessons.

Our piano—the same upright, I believe, on which my mother had practiced her own lessons as a girl—never stayed in tune for long. I do not remember the name of the maker; all I know is that it was not a Steinway, not a Baldwin, not a Chickering. It had a loud, bright, rather brassy sound which I prized from the start. On it, pianissimo was more difficult to manage than fortissimo, but in any case I preferred fortissimo. After I stopped taking lessons, the piano tuner no longer came around, a saving, but the neglect took its toll. The piano, with its darkening and chipped ivories, two or three of them glued back on slightly askew, went on sliding slowly downward out of tune, flatter and flatter, but unevenly flat from note to note. Some of the resulting combinations, different from month to month, used to fascinate me. I would strike some favorite dissonance repeatedly, thrilled by its oddness. How far its pitch had sunk overall came home to me when friends from the school band had to make dramatic adjustments to their horns to bring them into tune with our upright's B^b. Finally, it seemed to have settled into being almost exactly half a tone flat, resisting all efforts to make it hold a truer pitch. I can still remember the unique plangency of its B just below middle C (practically speaking, a B^b). The resonance of that note remains in my ear as a prototype of future resonances.

It was my friend Coney who encouraged me to ask for lessons again. He loved music. He liked picking out tunes and harmonies at our out-of-tune piano and had somehow taught himself to read music, probably with a clue or two from me. About my age, twelve or so, he needed lessons of his own, from a real teacher, but was shy about getting started and wanted company. We began lessons about the same time from Mrs. L., a neighbor, who wore long, colorful skirts and seemed almost to belong to the same generation as her own daughter. Thought to be separated from her husband, she augmented her doubtful income by offering lessons in dance as well, both ballroom and tap. Her daughter danced with fire and spirit and could play the piano with a certain brave flair, a living advertisement for her mother's skills. Coney lived a couple of blocks farther than I did from our teacher's house and along the way had to pass a small grocery. On lesson afternoons he could be seen hurrying down 19th Avenue, late as usual, a paper sack bulging with soft-drink bottles clutched against his chest. The bottles he would turn in at the grocery for the two-cent deposit on each. The proceeds paid for the week's lesson with Mrs. L.

I like to think that our experience was not unusual. Among the hundred thousand or so people in the Miami of the thirties there were probably a dozen other teachers like Mrs. L., if not more. And, in the nation at large, who can guess how many? Often there must have been a man in the background, whose chief stay and support the teacher was. During those moments in lessons when the eye begins to wander, the pupil might occasionally catch a glimpse of this mysterious figure, as I did once, though not at Mrs. L.'s. Outdoors he sat, in a sort of deck chair, under the shade of fruit trees, staring out across the half-mown grass at nothing at all. Did they drink, these lost men? Were they the victims of shellshock, or tuberculosis? Mrs. L.'s husband was none of these, but wrapped in a deeper mystery still. We saw little of him, for he was Hispanic and lived, as we pieced the story together, in Cuba. His visits were always brief, always unexpected. Suddenly he would be stepping off the bus that stopped at our corner. He was a small, fragile-looking person who carried himself stiffly and dressed in a black that seemed out of place in that climate. He sometimes carried a cane. Past one interested porch after another he would proceed, touching the tip of his cane gingerly to the sidewalk before him, like someone experimenting with the idea of blindness. A diplomat of sorts, or so we had been allowed to gather. Where the idea had come from that he showed up only to demand money from Mrs. L. I do not know. Perhaps at some point she had complained of this to my mother. In any case, we always suspected the worst of him, this courtly-looking little man who came and went like something in a dream.

It was not long before Coney and I found ourselves beyond Mrs. L.'s scope as a teacher. She must have known this time would come, and she remained sympathetic, interested in our future. Mrs. K. followed as my teacher. I used to ride my bicycle to her house, a mile or so distant. I would pedal through the sultry afternoons, working up to a furious speed and then coasting, no hands, music books balanced in the wire basket clipped to the handlebars. Mrs. K. herself could take me only so far into the piano literature— somewhere among the black keys of Chopin—but this proved to be about as far as I wanted to go at the time. The moods of the nocturnes and the ballades, dreamy and bittersweet, as they seemed then to me, were exactly right for someone just beginning to drift through the lovely-dark passages of adolescence. Sometimes I would move over on the piano bench for Mrs. K. to demonstrate her own interpretation of a certain passage. And the few bars might extend themselves all the way to the end of the piece, for at such times Mrs. K. was capable of forgetting herself. Transported, she would become another person. As the passionate notes of one or the other of the nineteenth-century Romantics, her specialty, sprang to life beneath her suddenly invigorated fingers, she seemed to rise briefly into some sphere of romance herself. Her tensed hands would rebound upward from the keys then, to quiver suspended above the final echoing chord, while she turned her head toward me and smiled, as if we shared a secret. Even as I returned the smile, she would be subsiding back into her ordinary self. This was not an illusion of mine. Clearly she felt something of it too, and this must have cast over her life a thin shadow of regret, the sort of mild discontent which adds a touch of mysterious interest to the characters of otherwise unexceptional persons. In the case of Mrs. K. the effect was purely transitory. Only when she was, so to speak, inspired by the miraculously rapid and precise movements of her own fingers, as if she herself hardly knew what was happening, did this second Mrs. K. rise to the surface, and then only for a few seconds at a time.

There seemed to be no one in Miami who could teach me what I really wanted to learn, which was how to compose music. Of course I was already composing what I could, obsessively. So was my friend Coney. We bought scorepaper at Amidon's Music Store downtown and filled it with thousands of notes, a form of magic. At fifteen I wrote a long piece grandly entitled "Myth" and intended for an orchestra larger than any I had yet heard. But when I inquired of Mrs. K. whom I could study composition with, she could come up with no names at all. She lent me her harmony textbook from the conservatory. That was a start, but limited, and I was looking for something vaster, more challenging. Sometimes I felt that no one had confidence in me but myself. There was my mother, but she would have believed in me without any reason to do so. A few years later— and, as I can't help feeling, too late, after the critical moment had passed—I was to meet the composer Carl Ruggles, Ives's friend, who wintered in Miami, and he very willingly took me on as a free pupil. Then, amply, the confidence which can be so important to the young was given me, and I must have become for a while proud and rather insufferable. Had I met Ruggles earlier I wonder if I might not now be writing music, very happily, whether in Hollywood (as I privately imagine) or in some academy or conservatory.

For several years I felt not so much lost as suspended in a vacuum. I had a sense of trying to make headway against some unseen obstacle, as in anxiety dreams. Meanwhile I read the books available in the public library. Teaching myself to read orchestral scores, I read through what there was of Haydn, Mozart, Beethoven; there was nothing in the library then so new as Debussy. It may be hard for anyone now to grasp how difficult recordings were to come by, and especially of new music. I remember listening for the first time to Stravinsky's *Firebird*, an orchestral commonplace now, and perhaps one already even then, though if so there was no way I could have known. With the sudden explosion of the whole orchestra at the start of the king's "infernal dance," I felt my face flush with excitement, there in the isolation of the listening booth. With a curious rightness this booth happened to be located on the mezzanine of the same department store in whose basement Mother and I had first encountered Mrs. Snow's rhythm band. (The name of the store had been changed to Richards' by then.) There too I first heard the other Stravinsky ballets and an early recording of Schoenberg's *Pierrot Lunaire*, featuring Erika Stiedry-Wagner, whom afterwards for years I was to remember wrongly as Erika Mann. (I was reading *The Magic Mountain* at the time and everything seemed to flow and fit together somehow.)

I wonder even now who in all of Miami could have purchased the single copy of the Schoenberg album, which stood for weeks unclaimed on the shelf. I could not afford to buy it myself, but I returned to it. Then one week it was gone. I knew better than to believe that it was meant for me alone, but I did think that no one else in the city—in the whole state of Florida, for that matter—could have appreciated it just then in the way I did. (I still believe that.) I knew better than to think the recording had been made for just that moment of revelation when I first touched needle to groove in the listening booth at Richards' and heard the high, harsh *Sprechstimme* ringing forth. I knew better once, but now I am not so sure.

STORIES

Little Elegy for Cello and Piano

I T   W A S   E A R L Y December, still warm. Damp leaves were packed thickly against the curbs that afternoon as we walked; others had stuck to the sidewalks or left their imprint there, a season's decalcomania.

Being early, we had time for a sort of tea at an outdoor café. It was just warm enough to sit outdoors under the canopy without discomfort, probably the last Sunday of the year when that would still be so. I remember the barely legible script of the oversized menus and the cheerful waitresses darting and hovering about in their starched sky-blue smocks. From time to time laughter arose from the tables around us.

There was a moment when Eugene folded his hand over my sister Florence's hand on the checkered tablecloth and smiled. When Eugene smiled broadly like that, it sometimes seemed to me that his domed bald head took on a slight glow as if lit up from inside. He and my sister had been married for more than thirty years, and it was clear that they had weathered out whatever storms had come their way. The waitress, bringing our hot cocoa and small pastries, took in the situation at a glance and beamed.

What we found to talk about I have forgotten. Someone unseen walked past on the sidewalk, whistling an odd little tune none of us could identify. It amused us, not to know. The aroma of Eugene's after-tea cigar blended with the smell of dregs and cake crumbs, of scrubbed bodies and clean clothes. The December sunshine continued to pour down. Overhead, beyond the canopy, the sky was cloudless.

We lingered. The service was cheerful and slow. We had to hurry, after all, through streets strangely empty. We passed a few of the lesser embassies, where little knots of people—journalists, we supposed—stood about waiting for someone to arrive or to depart. Per-

˙haps it was a day on which something important was expected, but if so I never learned what it was. At one of the embassies—I don't know Washington very well—a limousine did turn up the semicircular drive just as we reached the corner, and we stood for a moment watching while several dark-costumed persons were disgorged and swept indoors before any harm could be done to them.

By the time we had gone up the steps to the Phillips Collection, the foyer seemed crowded. Small groups were just beginning to drift toward the gallery where the chairs were set out for the afternoon's recital. Florence disappeared almost at once into the back room where her cello was. As we edged past the music stand and the open Steinway, two or three glances were cast in Eugene's direction. One of his pieces was on the program that afternoon, but Eugene was not widely enough known as a composer to be recognized by many. The Steinway gleamed. Eugene paused beside the open piano and stood looking down at his own reflection in the polished black of the wood.

We found seats, among the last untaken. They were in the corner next to the immense Bonnard, *La Grande Terrasse*. The painted couple in the bright foreground of the painting struck me at once as a couple a little like Florence and Eugene, but translated now into a sort of paradise made up all of flowers and light. One reason I had never passed beyond the amateur stage myself as a musician was a tendency I had to drift off, while listening, into my own fantasies. Except when actually at a keyboard playing, I could seldom attend to music as music for very long at a time, though I had always loved it. That afternoon I could see that the world of Bonnard would be an added temptation to drift.

I noted Florence, changed now into a long dark skirt, as she entered and executed her neat bow. The pianist, a small man with several large rings on his fingers, also bowed neatly and smiled. Behind them, at the other end of the room, the weakening sunlight filtered in through the narrow screens onto the bronze peacock and the slender reaching limbs of a potted plant on a table. With the first notes of the Fauré with which the performance began I could feel myself already wandering off down the painted terrace at my shoulder toward the sea and the sky with its gold and lavender clouds.

It was not till the half-moment of silence when the Fauré was done that I came to completely. I applauded with the rest. And now

I noticed a singular stillness descending on Eugene. His "Little Elegy for Cello and Piano" was next on the program. I saw how perfectly one could be tuned to listen. Eugene had become a listener; he was like some instrument made for that purpose. I could see his shoulders hunching, his breath drawing in. It is one of the ways I like to picture him. Then the piano began its little storm and almost as suddenly grew still. Florence's bow drew out a long note in the middle range and held it; and then, as she and the bejeweled pianist began their mournful dialogue, I saw Eugene's very jowls slacken with pleasure and contentment.

The piece was a sort of fantasia in one long movement. By *long* I mean ten or twelve minutes at most. But I had lost track of time. There was a perfect consonance between the Bonnard and Eugene's music. I thought I could read also on the faces of those nearest me a glow of attention that went beyond politeness or curiosity. And I sensed or imagined in Eugene himself a fulfillment which must come very rarely. Florence was bent close to her instrument, drawing from it the rich, exact sounds the composer had imagined, but now they took on an existence apart from him. They had momentarily a life in and of themselves, beyond us all.

At some point during the performance Eugene sneezed. There had been the usual muffled coughs and rustlings and shiftings all along, but the ear adjusts to familiar disruptions without difficulty. This sneeze of his was different. It obliterated one rapid little passage of notes, and I felt the loss more keenly than I could have explained at the time.

The last sounds drew me back from the terrace—three plucked chords repeated on the cello, quickly fading. Florence's familiar head with its bands of gray-piled hair remained bowed briefly over her cello, and she did not look up in our direction. Probably Eugene had asked her not to. For when heads began to swivel around in search of the composer, and a few swung our way, Eugene remained seated. He preferred his anonymity.

During intermission a number of his and Florence's musical friends from the area came over, and there was much pumping of hands. "Wonderful piece!" one friend exclaimed, and others joined in the praise.

I myself consider the "Little Elegy for Cello and Piano" to have been Eugene Bestor's masterpiece. Ten or twelve minutes of music, no more, but hardly to be improved upon—sad, regretful, complete. Yet it has not been heard since. Eugene died late that spring. Other works of the Bestor canon occasionally are heard, compositions longer established, but after the death of an artist one of two things generally happens. Either there is a rebirth of interest in his work, or else the general interest wanes and withers quickly. The latter is by far the more common case, and so it has been with Eugene's music, however much respected it once was.

There was a memorial recital, but Florence was not in the mood to attempt the "Little Elegy" again so soon. She may have considered the piece too close in spirit to the occasion. She wanted bright pieces only, and it was her choice. Then, too, she may have wondered a little, as I did at the time, whether Eugene had had some early hint or premonition of his death to come, whether he might not have written the piece, in a sense, for himself.

Two or three years later I learned from a program Florence mailed me that the "Little Elegy" was to be done at a college in Vermont near which the Bestors had lived. She knew my high opinion of the work. It was probably included on her initiative, for she was the featured performer of the evening. But as luck would have it, she fell ill a day or two before the performance and the program had to be canceled at the last minute. Apparently it was a hard-luck piece, a jinx perhaps, as certain plays are said to be. Florence herself, I know, never again played it in public, and now she is gone also.

The Bestor manuscripts have come down to me. One day, I suppose, the library of the college in Vermont will have them. I used to take out the manuscript of Eugene's final composition now and then and let my eye run over the spidery calligraphy of the notes. The small black notes climbed the staves slowly or floated above the top line like miniature storm clouds. There was a visual drama in this, and I had enough training to hear faintly the skeletal sounds behind the notes. But the music was a little beyond my practical skills. I could pick out the notes of the piano part at my own pace and work up the difficult passages, but it was not the same as performing it. In any case, there was not a cellist—none I had heard of anyhow—in the entire sprawling range of the sun-and-sand community I had by then retired to. Perhaps there would have been one at the nearest junior college, but that was miles away, back across the causeway.

There comes a time of day now when I sit back and listen to the surf. It is too far away to be seen, but I can hear it. The sun is easing its way down, scattering color. There is a terrace of my own out there, made of bricks, with potted palm tree and potted orange tree. I can hear the music better where I sit than at the keyboard. I wonder sometimes how many others who were present in the Phillips that afternoon could still summon up any of the by now broken web of sounds produced then, as I am able to do, though of course only partially and just barely. The last three plucked chords—surely the sound of them hangs on, consciously or not, in the memory of a few others, though fading.

There is one phrase of the cello's—an early phrase, before the sounds had become mixed up in my mind with Bonnard's colors—which holds fast for me, a little upward rush and subsiding of notes that has come to represent some nameless feeling which otherwise has no voice or expression. This is the way it is written out in the manuscript:

A brief inhaling and exhaling, a somewhat drawn-out deep gasp or sigh. Sometimes this phrase comes to me just as I am falling asleep. It is not exactly that I hear it. It is just there, and I do not of course know what it means.

It is sentimental of me to think of Eugene as surviving through this fragment, which in any case I am probably the only person anywhere to remember. And yet it does seem as if all the hard early years of study and practice here and abroad, the thousands of mornings of seclusion in his studio, the remarkable ear, the near-photographic memory and recall, had all come down to this, this one ghostly phrase. And soon there will be no one at all to remember how even these six notes sounded.

The Artificial Moonlight

Coconut Grove, 1958

1

THE LANGS, Hal and his wife Julie, were giving a party. From the screen porch of their apartment you could see the colored lights of the neighborhood sailing club strung out across the bay and farther out the bulky shadows of the members' boats riding at anchor. Often, with nightfall, there would be a breeze. As it came up from the bay and across the bayshore road past the shaggy royal palms bordering the driveway, it cooled the Langs' porch like a large and efficient fan.

But tonight there was no breeze at all. It was past midnight, and still the apartment felt oppressive and close. The heat was spoiling the party. It was a going-away party for an old friend of the Langs', Jack Felton. They saw him now only when he came home from graduate school to visit his parents. In a day or two, with summer over, he would be taking off for Europe on a Fulbright. Now some vague melancholy of departure and change seemed to be settling over everyone and everything.

In the back room a record player was turning, unattended. Sounds of old jazz drifted out to the porch. The casual guests, the friends of friends, had gone home. The few who remained looked settled in for the night. They looked listless and bored, some on the sagging wicker chair and settee, some on the floor cushions brought out from the stuffy back rooms. They looked as though they might never move again, not even to flip the stack of records when the music ended.

2

If anyone did, it would probably be Julie herself. Of the Langs, Julie was the dependable one. Five afternoons a week she worked as a legal stenographer, while her husband kept up appearances by giving occasional painting lessons to the daughters of tourists. There might be an occasional shortage of money, but otherwise they lived with as much freedom from care and nearly as much leisure as the well-to-do. Approaching their thirties, they seemed as perpetually youthful as movie stars. The odd hours they kept could be hard on Julie, and occasionally she retired early. She would be so wound up that she could not sleep and would have to read for a long time before her eyes closed. It was an intense sort of reading that went beyond simple pleasure. One .wall of their bedroom was filled with books, and when they made love without turning the lights off she sometimes caught herself letting her eyes rove across the titles on the spines of the larger books. Hal had complained of this publicly, to her embarrassment, but she seemed unable to change.

Alone in their bedroom, reading or not, she liked the sound of conversation as it floated back late at night from the porch. It was soothing, like the quiet washing sound of an ocean. It was hot, and there was a little fan she could reach out for and turn on, but she did not often use it. She liked the warm weather; she could not imagine living anywhere but Miami.

Some nights Julie felt left out of things. Their friends all drank, and, except for very special occasions, Julie did not. But there was more than that to the feeling. She would begin to suspect them of planning something exciting and daring from which she was to be excluded. However unreasonable it might be, there was nothing she could do about the feeling. Julie gazed now with half-closed eyes across the porch at her husband, where he sat perched on one arm of the old wicker settee, bending down to speak to a tall blond woman in slacks. She knew she would never be able to trace this feeling of hers back to its source. How far back would she have to go? She was an orphan, adopted by a couple old enough to be her grandparents, long ago dead. Could it be as simple as that? She thought sometimes that she must have Spanish blood. That would account for her dark coloring, for her thick black eyebrows, her almost blue-black hair, which only a few days before she had cut short, over Hal's objections.

In the back room now the record stopped and another dropped down from the stack. Julie did not recognize the tune, which was slow and bluesy. Shutting her eyes, she took a sip of the plain orange juice in her glass and, leaning back, crossed her legs. Ellington, she guessed; Duke Ellington. One small sandaled foot, the nails that afternoon painted a deep bloodred for the party, commenced to swing nervously back and forth, back and forth.

3

Jack wondered if the others were waiting for him to take some initiative. After all, the party was for him.

Whenever he came back home now it was as if the curtain had risen on a new act; the actors were the same as before, but the playwright had revised the plot. It might be impossible to point to a time when everything had been as it was meant to be, but that time must have existed once. They all felt it. Lately to Jack every change—the divorce of one couple, the moving away of another—came as an unwelcome change.

Jack knew that he seemed quieter now than in the past. In fact, he *was* quieter. In some small way, just as he could imagine his friends might do, he had begun to miss his old self. He sat now very quietly, stretched out on his floor cushion, leaning back against the wall, his long legs folded in a lazy tangle before him. He looked half-asleep. But behind his glasses his eyes were open. He might have been listening to the music, except that the music had stopped.

He had intended to listen. He had stacked the records himself, old favorites of his. Then, just as the music had begun to bear him back toward the past, it had come to him suddenly why the girl sitting beside him, to whom he had been talking desultorily for the last twenty minutes or so, was wearing so loose and unbecoming a blouse—tardily, for she was visibly pregnant. To Jack, who had known her for years, the realization came hard. When those very records were being cut, this girl, Susan, had been listening obediently to the nuns of her grammar school, wearing the blue-and-white uniform Jack remembered. The summer before, when he had last seen her, Susan had not been married. And already now her husband, Robert or Bob, the sallow, sleepy-looking fellow in the corner, who never had much to say, had got her pregnant.

For the time being Jack could concentrate on nothing but this, this fact that to him seemed so absolutely, if mysteriously, wrong.

4

Hal was bending down, whispering into the blond woman's ear. There was nothing important to be said, but he would not have minded if the others thought there was. He took pleasure in merely leaning toward her in a way that involved some momentary illusion of intimacy.

What he said was: "The vodka's about to run out." Then he sighed.

A sort of perfume seemed to be coming from a spot just behind the woman's ear. Green was her married name, Karen Green, and Hal had known her longer than he had known his wife. In high school he had had a hopeless crush on her, but never before had he noticed how peculiarly large and yet shapely her left ear was, from which the hair was drawn back, and how many little whorls it contained, impossible to count. Was she wearing her hair some new way?

Hal leaned closer. "Of course we could always go out to Fox's for more. More vodka."

It was half a question. It was the tone he always fell into with Karen, a tone of casual flirtation, just as though they were still in school together.

5

A rustling stirred in the palms outside, the first sign of something like a breeze. The rolled tarpaulins high up on the tall screened windows seemed to catch their breath.

They could hear a dance band playing, not very far away, the sounds of a rumba band carried on the breeze—snarling trumpet, bongo drums, maracas. Had it been playing all this time? Everyone listened. Jack straightened up and peered about the room, somewhat crossly, like a person roused from an interesting dream.

"The Legion dance!" someone called out.

The large, good-looking man, who from his cushion beside Julie Lang's chair had also been watching Hal and the blond woman, climbed to his feet. This was Sid Green, Karen's husband. Standing, he loomed larger than anyone else in the group.

He called across the porch, "Hey, Hal, you by any chance a member?" His voice sounded louder to him than he had intended.

"For Christ's sake, Sid, the *Foreign* Legion maybe, not the American."

"I mean if somebody was a member, we could go to the dance," Sid said. "If anybody wanted to. I mean we can't just sit here." "Crash it?" the pregnant girl asked.

"Oh, maybe not," Sid said, looking around. His flash of enthusiasm was fading.

"I don't know," Hal said, with a glance at Sid's wife beside him. "Oh, let's do go!" Julie cried out suddenly from across the porch. "For God's sake, let's do something! Just wait a second till I change my shoes." Kicking her sandals off, fluffing her short crop of hair out as she went, she hurried back through the dark apartment toward the bedroom.

6

But when she returned she saw at once that something was wrong. Hal and Karen were missing, and Jack as well. Julie peered into the corner where the other women were sitting—Susan and a girl named Annabelle, who appeared to be sound asleep.

"Aren't you coming?" Julie asked nervously.

"Not me," Susan said, placing one hand on her stomach. "Not in my condition." Her husband beside her beamed and said nothing.

Julie had never had children, and she was a good deal older than Susan, seven or eight years at least, but there was really no reason for her to feel uncomfortable about it. Everyone knew that she did not want children, that she preferred her freedom.

She turned to Sid; their eyes met. He was not amusing, as Hal and even Jack could be, but he was very good-looking in his athletic way, dark and mysterious. They knew very little about Sid; he withheld himself. They said that his family had money, but was it true? If only, Julie thought, he would volunteer himself more, like Hal. But at least Sid could be managed.

"Come on, you," she said, taking him by the hand and pulling. "Let's catch up with the others."

Sid allowed himself to be led out the door.

7

On the dock it was quiet. Only stray phrases of the Cuban trumpet carried out that far.

When they had stepped down onto the dock, which was floated on an arrangement of large painted oil drums, it had bobbed and swayed with every step. By now it had settled down. The three of them—Hal and Karen and Jack—sat dangling their legs over the end, looking out at the anchored boats rocking on the water. Above the water, very bright, as if left over from some festivity, were strung the lights of the sailing club. All of the lights together cast a strange glow on the dark waters of the bay, a thin swath of artificial moonlight which reached out perhaps halfway toward the long, indistinct blur of the nearest island.

Jack wanted to touch the water, see how cold it was. He set the drink he had brought with him down carefully upon the planking and removed his loafers.

Not that he meant to swim. But as he put one leg down and his toes touched water, which was not as cold as expected, he found himself thinking of a woman they all knew, a woman named Roberta, who had once lived in the apartment above the Langs. She used sometimes to swim out to the island, which was no more than a dark, low line on the horizon. There was nothing to do out there; it was a mere piney arm of sand. She would wait long enough to catch her breath and then swim back. That was all. It would not have been, if you were a swimmer, very dangerous. There were plenty of boats along the way to catch hold of if you tired.

They all seemed to be thinking of Roberta just then, for when Hal asked, out of the blue, if they knew that Roberta was in San Francisco, Karen said, "Funny, I was just thinking of that time she drove her car into the bay."

"Well, not quite all the way in," Hal said. "It stalled, you know."

Hal was the authority on the stories they told about people they used to know. There were a lot of them, and they had been told so often that the facts had become subject to endless small revisions and adjustments.

"I thought it was a palm tree that stopped her," Jack commented, rather sourly. He had never been one of Roberta's admirers. At the time, she had seemed a silly romantic girl, mad for attention. He tried to recall her face. He remembered it now as pale and moon-shaped, but perhaps that was someone else's, someone still more elusive.

"You're right," Hal agreed. "There was a palm tree somewhere, but where?" He began to reconstruct. "The car must have caromed off the palm and gone on into the bay. Well, partway in. I seem to picture it as hanging over the edge, sort of."

"I always thought she did it on purpose," Karen said.

"No, it was an accident." On that point Hal was definite.

Gradually a pleasant melancholy settled over them. All around, the small dinghies moored to the dock nosed up against the wood. One was painted a vivid orange and white, the colors of the sailing club. A car passed behind them along the bayshore road, heading for Miami proper.

Karen looked out across the bay. "Well, she should have done it on purpose. That would have made sense. It would have been—oh, I don't know . . . It would have *meant* something."

8

Off and on all evening Jack had wondered what, if anything, was understood between Hal and Karen. Karen was very beautiful, more beautiful than she had been ten years ago, just out of high school, when everyone, himself and Hal too, was buzzing around her. Experience had only ripened her; she made him think of some night-blooming flower the neighbors call you out to see. Probably just then—at that very minute, Jack wanted to believe—she was at the absolute peak of her beauty. Next summer, surely by the summer after, she would have crossed the line they were all approaching. On the other side of that line strangers would no longer find her quite so remarkable to look at, only old friends like Hal and himself, who would remember her face as it had been once, caught in the light of a driftwood fire at some beach picnic or other, or more likely as it was now, shaped by the glow of the lights strung out from the dock over the water.

He recalled a story of Hal's about how Hal and a girl Jack did not know had rowed out to the island one night and stayed till dawn. Thinking about the story now, with the island itself so near, Jack began to feel curiously giddy, as if the dock were starting to bob again.

"What about the island?" he asked.

"What about it?" Karen said.

"What about going out to the island?"

"I couldn't swim that far," she said. "Not nearly."

"Not swim. We borrow one of these dinghy things. Ask Hal. He's done it before."

Hal grinned. "Right. The night watchman, he sleeps back in that little shack. Besides, he doesn't really give a damn."

In a moment they were climbing down into the orange-and-white dinghy. This was a trickier operation than it looked. Whenever one of them put a foot down, exploring, the boat seemed to totter almost to the point of capsizing. Jack could not hold back a snort of laughter.

"Shh," Hal said.

"I thought he didn't give a damn," Karen said, tittering.

"Shh," Jack said. "Shh."

Once they were all seated, Hal took up the oars. They were just casting off, Jack had just managed to slip the rope free, when they heard footsteps coming up the walk. The rope dropped with a splash.

"Hey, we see you down there," a voice called, and Karen recognized it as her husband's. Just behind him stood Julie. Their shadows were bent out over the water.

"Shh," Karen hissed. Already the current was bearing them out, and there was a wide dark patch between boat and dock.

"Come on back."

"Can't. Current's got us."

Hal managed to plant one oar firmly in the water, and with that the boat began to turn in a slow circle.

"How was the dance?" Hal called politely.

For reply Julie stamped her foot on the dock. "Come on back," she called.

"Aw, Julie, I sincerely want to know how it was."

"Now, Hal, stop it."

"Actually they were very nice about it," Sid said, "but we felt kind of out of place."

"I feel kind of out of place right here," said Jack, dizzy with the motion of the boat.

"Oh, you're all drunk," Julie said. "Every one of you is hopelessly drunk and besotted."

9

It ended with Sid and Julie untying another dinghy and climbing into it. Quietly then the two boats glided out with the mild current through the lighted water.

Under the lights Jack felt like an escaping prisoner caught in the beam of a spotlight, and he closed his eyes, distinctly giddy now. When he looked again, they were already emerging from the shadows of the anchored boats into the clear space beyond, where it was dark. The other boat was no longer in sight. Hal feathered the oars, and they drifted with the flow, letting Sid and Julie catch up. It was very still. They could hear Sid grunting over the oars before they saw his dinghy coming up, gaining fast. In the dark his bent-over shape looked like part of the ghostly, gliding boat.

Their eyes had become used to the dark, and they were near enough now to make out ahead the narrow strip of sand edged with stunted pines that marked the shore of the island. A moment later the outline of a landing pier with several large nets spread out to dry on skeletal frames came into sight. Hal pointed the boat that way and resumed rowing.

The pier was rickety but looked safe enough. When Hal leaped out, the others followed.

10

Karen lived with the vaguely troubling impression that someone, some man, had all her life been leaning toward her, about to touch her. It was like a dream. Instinctively she wanted to draw back but could not. Just now, as they were all lying on the little beach of the island, Hal had leaned toward her to whisper something about exploring the island farther down, around the point, and she had consented without a thought. Tomorrow, thinking back over it to excuse herself, she might come to believe that Hal had meant for the others to join them, but now, when it was still quite clear in her mind, she knew that that was not true. She did not understand why she had come. Karen was not in any way angry with her husband, and she had never felt the least sexual interest in Hal, who was simply an old friend.

Her earliest recollection of Hal was of a brash, rebellious boy in high school, a loud talker, but solitary, whom she had seen once standing alone after classes at the end of a long corridor puffing away at—of all things!—a cigar, as if he were already grown up. Perhaps that was why she had come away with him now, that memory. Hal had looked up from the end of the corridor and seen her watching him puff away at the forbidden cigar, but neither had spoken at the time, nor, for that matter, had either mentioned the incident since.

Karen was not certain that Hal would remember it. Even if he did not, Karen wondered if what had started then, however slight it was, might not have led in some unforeseeable way to this. They had got around the point now from the beach where the others were lying, but an occasional murmur of voices still drifted their way.

Hal had taken her hand to lead her across one stretch of slippery rocks, but he had not otherwise touched her. He was talking softly and at incredible length about a book he was reading, a novel about some boys marooned on an island. Of all things! Karen thought. Of all things! She had failed to catch the novelist's name, and the conversation by now was too far advanced to ask. Hal seemed to have reached the point of criticizing the style of the writer. *Seemed*— she could not really say. Her attention was failing, fading. She could picture herself standing just where she stood now but at the same time disappearing out over the water, which was dark and astonishingly calm.

In the distance she heard Sid's laughter. She had the most vivid sensation of his anxiety and of Julie's as well. She wished she could do something about it, but Hal's voice going on and on endlessly about the novel she would never read was fixing her, or a part of her, to a certain point, pinning her there, draining her of all power, while the rest of her drifted out, out . . . If only Sid would raise his voice and call her! She remembered the after-supper games of hide-and-seek as a child with her large family of sisters and a brother. One game counted among her most persistent memories; it recurred in her dreams. She was crouching behind a prickly bush on the lawn of her parents' house. She was the last one of the sisters not yet found by her brother, who was "It," and she could hear her brother's footsteps coming through the dusk and his voice calling, almost whispering, "Karen? Karen? Karen?" And she ran to him and threw her arms around him, whereupon her brother, who was years older and much larger than she, lifted her from the ground and swung her around and around until they both fell to the grass, overcome with laughter and relief.

How tired she was! She wanted Hal to stop talking. She wanted him to touch her; she wanted whatever was going to happen to begin. And yet she could not bring herself to say to him that it would be all right, that whatever he did or did not do scarcely mattered.

11

Jack woke from a sound sleep feeling cold. He was alone. He sat up and listened for some sound to indicate where the others were. Except for the water that was licking up along the sand almost to his feet and out again, the silence was complete. Where had they gone? He assumed that they were off exploring the island, probably by twos, but what it all added up to he no longer much cared. His curiosity, brimming not long before, had gone flat.

Somewhere he had misplaced his glasses. He groped in the sand for them near where he had been sleeping, but without luck. He sat blinking out across the water into the sky, where the first streaks and patches of light were beginning to show. He felt reluctant to get up and start looking for the others. He did not like the idea of stumbling across them in the dark, half-blind as he was. He hardly cared if he ever saw any of them again. His stomach felt a little queasy, but he was not sure if it was from drinking. In any case, he had been through worse.

Only after he made his way back along the path to the landing pier and saw that the boats were missing did he realize what had happened. They had left him behind; they had abandoned him on the island.

At first he was simply angry. He peered as well as he could toward land. The sailing-club lights were still burning over the water. That he could see, but no farther. It was beginning to get light, and soon, he knew, the night watchman would wake up and turn the lights off. Already the lights were beginning to look superfluous. What a stupid joke this was, he thought. He imagined the story they would make out of it—the night they marooned Jack on the island! For a moment he considered the chance of swimming back, like Roberta. If he could make seventy or eighty yards on his own, there would be plenty of boats to hang onto. But the water looked cold, and his stomach was too unsettled.

Cold after the warmth of the night, he wrapped his arms around his shoulders. He felt as alone as he could remember ever having felt, and in an unfamiliar place, a place he could not even, without his glasses, see clearly, all fuzzy and vague. Any minute his teeth would start chattering. Standing there like that, realizing how foolish and pointless it was, for he was nearly sober by then, he began to call out their names as loudly as he could, one after the other, a kind of angry roll call—*Hal, Sid, Karen, Julie!* He had no idea how far his voice carried over the water, and in any case there was no answer. At last he sat down on the rickety pier and began to wait for someone to come and rescue him. And gradually, sitting there, shivering with the morning cool, Jack reflected, absurdly enough, that he would be the hero of whatever story came to be told of the night. He had been singled out. At once he began to feel better about the evening. The party—it had not been a dead loss, after all. He found himself almost forgiving them for having abandoned him; eventually he would probably forgive them, forgive them entirely and for everything, whatever they had done or not done. Without him, whatever had happened—and he did not want to know yet what that was, afraid that his new and still fragile sense of the evening might evaporate once he knew—would not have happened. In some way, he was responsible. In any case, he would have forgiven them a great deal—laughter, humiliation, even perhaps betrayal—as they would forgive him practically anything. He saw all that now. Well, it was a sentimental time of night—the very end of it—and he had had a lot to drink, but he was willing to believe that the future would indeed be bleak and awful without such friends, willing to take their chance with you, ready even to abandon you on a chunk of sand at four A.M. for nothing but the sheer hell of it. And he was, for the moment, remarkably contented.

Brighton, 1980

12

The apartment building the Langs had lived in had been gone since the late sixties. There had been a boom. The fine old house— one of the oldest in the area, one to which Indians before the turn of the century had come up across the bay in their canoes to trade— had lasted as long as any, but it had succumbed in the end to time and money. No matter, it would have been dwarfed by the new high-rises looming around it. On its site stood one of the poshest of the latest generation of high-rises, expensive and grand, with glass and impractical-looking small balconies painted in three bold colors. It had been and was still a grand site, with a marvellous sweeping view of the bay, the little masted boats thick on the water, like blown leaves.

143

It was the people who concerned Jack more; he knew none of the new people. In his own place, when he went there now, he felt uncomfortable and alien.

One day—more than twenty years had passed—sitting in a flat in Brighton, England, looking idly out over the gray, disturbed sea in a direction he thought must be toward home, Jack began making a sort of mental catalogue of all his friends from that period. He had not thought it out in advance. The idea just came to him, and he began. He wanted to try to remember everyone who was together at a certain time in the old life, at a precise moment even, and the night of his going-away party came back to him.

The list began with Susan's son, the one she had been pregnant with at the time. Jack was pleased with himself for having thought to include her child-to-be in his recollection. She never had another. The son, he had heard, was a tall, intelligent boy, off at college somewhere, no trouble to anybody. Jack had not seen him since the boy started grammar school. The boy's name he no longer remembered.

The sallow husband—Robert or Bob—had been some trouble or had some trouble. Drinking? Whatever had caused his silence, he had sunk deeper into it over the years. Eventually he had found his way back north to Philadelphia, into his father's business, a chain of liquor stores. Just the thing, Jack thought now, just the thing.

Susan herself owned a small stucco house in the Grove, almost hidden by shrubs and palms and jacarandas. Her time seemed to go into nothing at all, unless it was a little gardening. She had no time for anything, certainly not for friends, and rarely ventured out. She kept a few cats; their number grew.

The great surprise was Sid, the only one to have become famous. Not exactly famous, Jack acknowledged, but well-known. No one had sensed the power and ambition hidden in Sid back then, certainly not Karen. From small starts, from short sailing trips down into the Keys, later out to the Bahamas, Sid had taken the great dare of a long solo sail across the Atlantic, kept a journal, and published an account of the voyage. Modestly popular. Later, other adventures, other books. He was married now to a minor movie actress or ex-actress, still quite beautiful—a brunette, not at all like Karen in appearance—and they lived most of the year in southern France. (It was true—his family had had some money.) Jack had recently had occasion to call on them and found that he enjoyed the visit immensely. Sid had become voluble, a great smiler—of all of them, the most thoroughly and happily changed.

Karen, on the other hand, had been through three more husbands. Two daughters, one of them married, with a daughter of her own. It seemed incredible to Jack that Karen should have become a grandmother. It was like a magic trick, seen but not believed. Sometimes, of an evening, as they sat talking over a drink beside the current husband's pool, the bug light sending out its intermittent little zap, he had caught a sidelong glimpse of the former Karen, a Karen absolute and undiminished, still slender, seemingly remote, cool if not cold, not to be found out. Some secret she had, and it had kept her beautiful. Her present husband was often ill, and there was a bad look around her own eyes. She looked away from you much of the time. She had never done anything of any importance in her life, and everybody had always loved her for herself alone. What happiness!

Julie, as she had wished, had never had any children. Over the years she had gone a little to corpulence, but her foot, dainty as ever, still swung back and forth to some nervous rhythm of her own. She, who had always abhorred and fled from the cold, ran a bookstore now in Boston. She had become an expert on books. The way Jack had of explaining this to himself—he had browsed in her shop once or twice when in Boston—was simply that she had always been a reader. Those nights Hal had been out catting around she had read. She had read and read and she had always loved books and, in the end, it had come to this. She seemed satisfied.

Nor was Hal—the great romantic, Hal—a totally lost cause, even though he had, in his maturity, held down a steady job, the same job now for ten or eleven years, easily a record for him. He managed a gallery. He was right for it, a gallery in the Grove popular with everyone, wealthy tourists especially. It also provided him the contacts with women he seemed to need—wives, daughters, perhaps even a youthful grandmother or two. Women, young and old, some beautiful, some rich, pursuing Hal, who was not getting any younger. He let his colorful shirts hang out over a slight belly, wore dark glasses much of the time, rode out his hangovers with good grace and considerable experience. He still painted, obsessively detailed work, with clear jeweled colors, almost Byzantine. He sold everything he made and never set too high a price. He was as happy as he deserved to be, perhaps happier. Not married—it was better that way. Some nights he liked being alone.

Several of his friends, Jack realized, were actually happy. The shape of their futures must always have been there, just as eye color is built into the chromosomes at birth; impossible to read, all the same, except backward. The night of the party had been a sort of key perhaps, and it should have been clear then that the Langs would never last, not as a couple, and if the Langs went, then the Greens were another doubtful case; and something in the way her husband had cast his silent, wary, unfathomable glances at the pregnant Susan might have hinted at trouble ahead for them as well. Now no one was married to the right person. No one, as Jack saw it, would ever be married to the right person again. The time when everything was exactly as it should be would always really be some other time, but back then, that summer, it had seemed very close.

From the window of the flat he could see only a little corner of the sea, and he wanted, for some reason, to be closer to the water. Dressing warmly, Jack walked down to the parade, braced himself against the cold blowing wind and walked and walked, for forty minutes or so. He found himself down on the shingle, almost alone there. It was too nasty a day for people to be out. A big boat hung on the horizon. Jack thought back to the beach of the sandy little bay island. Here in this foreign place he saw himself again on a little island, isolated, the last civilized speck, himself against a faceless and unpredictable world. Jack felt like calling out again the names of his friends, but of course he did not. He tried to remember how he had been rescued that other time, who it was that had come out in a dinghy for him, risking the wrath of the sleepy night watchman. Probably Sid. Julie had cooked a nice breakfast—he remembered that. No one would be coming to rescue him now, not that he needed rescuing or wanted rescuing, even in the sort of half-dreaming state he had fallen into. But the thought did occur to him, in passing.

CRITICISM

Meters and Memory

T H E   M N E M O N I C   value of meters seems always to have been recognized. There are, to begin with, the weather saws, counting spells, and the like, which one does more or less get by heart in childhood. But any ornament, however trivial and even meaningless, probably assists the recollection to some degree, if by ornament we mean a device of sound or structure not required by the plain sense of a passage. Repetition obviously functions in this way—anaphora, refrains, even the sort of repetition which involves nothing more than an approximate equivalence of length, as in Pound's Sapphic fragment:

> Spring . . . .
> Too long . . . . . .
> Gongula . . . . . .

Likewise with such structural features as parallel parts or syllogistic order, whether in verse or prose. For that matter, fine and exact phrasing alone enables the memory to take hold about as well as anything. A friend of mine, at parties, preferred to recite prose rather than verse, usually, as I recall, the opening paragraph of *A Farewell to Arms*.

The purely mnemonic character of a passage, however, appears to contribute little to its esthetic power. Often enough rhymes are more effective mnemonically than meters, and occasionally other devices may prove to be. But the meters, where employed at all, are likely to be the groundwork underlying other figurations, hence basic, if not always dominant. Consider a couplet like "Red sky at morning, / Sailor take warning." Here the meters cooperate with the rhymes to fit the lines to one another, not only as lines of verse but as linked parts of a perception. It is no more than a slight exaggeration to claim that the couplet becomes fixed in memory by reason of this sense of fittedness. But few devices of sound are enough in themselves to ensure recall. Should, for example, the sky of the couplet be changed from red to blue, although neither rhyme nor meter would be affected, I cannot believe the couplet would survive. Survival in this case has something to do with aptness of observation, with use, that is, as well as cleverness or beauty. The kernel of lore provides a reason for keeping the jingle: the jingle preserves the lore in stable form.

Now all this is to consider memory, as is customary, from the viewpoint of an audience, as if a significant purpose of poetry were simply to put itself in the way of being memorized. For my part, when I am at work on a poem, the memory of an audience concerns me less than my own. While the meters and other assorted devices may ultimately make the lines easier for an audience to remember, they are offering meanwhile, like the stone of the sculptor, a certain resistance to the writer's efforts to call up his subject, which seems always to be involved, one way or another, with memory. (Hobbes somewhere calls imagination the same thing as memory.) In any case, memory is going to keep whatever it chooses to keep not just because it has been made easy and agreeable to remember but because it comes to be recognized as worth the trouble of keeping, and first of all by the poet. The audience will find it possible to commit to memory only what the poet first recalls for himself. Anything can be memorized, including numbers, but numbers that refer to something beyond themselves, as to the combination of a safe, are the easier to keep in mind for that reason. Something other than themselves may likewise be hidden in the meters, and an aptness to be committed to memory might almost be taken as a sign of this other presence. Pattern is not enough. The trivial and insignificant pass beyond recall, no matter how patterned, discounting perhaps a double handful of songs and nonsense pieces,* where the pattern itself has somehow become a part of what is memorable. But such a result is exceptional. What happens in the more serious and ordinary case is that some recollection of a person, of an incident or a landscape, whatever we are willing to designate as subject, comes to seem worth preserving. The question for the poet is how to preserve it.

---

*Nonsense may be the condition, in any case, to which devices of sound in themselves aspire.

One motive for much if not all art (music is probably an exception) is to accomplish this—to keep memorable what deserves to be remembered. So much seems true at least from the perspective of the one who makes it. Nor should any resemblance to the more mechanical functions of camera and tape recorder prove embarrassing: like a literary text in the making, film and tape also permit editing, room enough for the artist. Let emotion be recollected, in tranquillity or turmoil, as luck and temperament would have it. And then what? Art lies still in the future. The emotion needs to be fixed, so that whatever has been temporarily recovered may become as nearly permanent as possible, allowing it to be called back again and again at pleasure. It is at this point that the various aids to memory, and meter most persistently, begin to serve memory beyond mnemonics. Such artifices are, let us say, the fixatives. Like the chemicals in the darkroom, they are useful in developing the negative. The audience is enabled to call back the poem, or pieces of it, the poet to call back the thing itself, the subject, all that was to become the poem.

The transcription of experience represented by the meters ought not to be confused with the experience itself. At best the meters can perform no more than a re-enactment, as on some stage of the mind. This being so, to object to the meters as unnatural because unrealistic is to miss the point. Like the odd mustaches and baggy pants of the old comedians, they put us on notice that we are at a certain distance from the normal rules and expectations of life. The effect has been variously called a distancing or a framing. Wordsworth described it as serving "to divest language in a certain degree of its reality, and thus to throw a sort of half consciousness of unsubstantial existence over the whole composition." The meters signify this much at least, that we are at that remove from life which traditionally we have called art.

Their very presence seems to testify to some degree of plan, purpose, and meaning. The meters seem always faintly teleological by implication, even in company with an anti-teleological argument, as the case may be. They are proof of the hand and ear of a maker (uncapitalized), even in a poetry which otherwise effaces the self. They seem to propose that an emotion, however uncontrollable it may have appeared originally, was not, in fact, unmanageable. "I don't know why I am crying" becomes "Tears, idle tears, I know not what they mean." The difference seems important to me. The poetic line comes to constitute a sort of paraphrase of the raw feeling, which will only get broken back down close to its original state in some future critic's reparaphrase. The writer in meters, I insist, may feel as deeply as the nonmetrical writer, and the choice whether or not to use meters is as likely to be dictated by literary fashion as by depth of feeling or sincerity. Nevertheless, they have become a conventional sign for at least the desire for some outward control; though their use cannot be interpreted as any guarantee of inner control, the very act of writing at all does usually imply an attempt to master the subject well enough to understand it, and the meters reinforce the impression that such an attempt is being made and perhaps succeeding. Even so, the technology of verse does not of itself affirm a philosophy, despite arguments to the contrary. Certain recent critics have argued that even syntax is now "bogus," since the modern world contains no such order as that implied in an ordinary sentence, much less a metrical one. But the imitation theory underlying this argument seems naive and unhistorical to me, for it was never the obligation of words or of word-order to imitate conditions so reflexively. Syntax deals, after all, primarily with word-order, not world-order, and even the meters, or so it seems to me, can imitate only by convention.

Let me take a simple case. Yvor Winters once offered his line, "The slow cry of a bird," as an example of metrical imitation, not strictly of a birdcall itself but of "the slowness of the cry." The convention would seem to be that two or more strong syllables in succession carry associations of slowness and heaviness, while two or more weak syllables in succession carry contrary associations of rapidity and lightness: melancholy on the one hand, playfulness on the other. But the displacement of a stress from *of* to *cry* in the Winters line, bringing two stresses together, fails to slow the line down, as I hear it. Substitute for this "The *quick* cry of a bird," and the two weak syllables following *cry* can be said to do as much to speed the line up, or as little. But whether the cry is to sound quick or slow, the metrical situation itself remains, practically speaking, identical. If any question of interpretation arises from the reversed foot, the meaning of the reversal must depend on the denotation of the adjective rather than on the particular arrangement of syllables and stresses, for denotation overrides any implication of the meters apart from it. Though apparently agreed on by generations of poets, the minor convention on which Winters was depending is hardly observed any longer except in criticism or occasionally the classroom. Nor was it, for that matter, observed by Milton in his great melancholy-playful pair, "Il Penseroso" and "L'Allegro," or if observed, then only to be consciously played against. Composers of music for the movies learned early that direct imitation of a visual image through sound was best restricted to comic effects (pizzicati, trombone glissandi, staccato bassoons). Pushed far enough, and that is not very far at all, the results of metrical imitations can seem similarly cartoonlike:

> I sank to the pillow, and Joris, and he;
> I slumbered, Dirck slumbered, we slumbered all three.*

In any case, simple imitation by means of rhythm would seem to be more plausible in free verse, with its greater flexibility, and most workable in prose, which is allowed any and every arrangement of syllables. The point seems obvious and incontrovertible to me, though never brought up in quite this way, I think. Wordsworth ascribes to the meters a different and greater power, finding in them a "great efficacy in tempering and restraining the passion by an intertexture of ordinary feeling," and, he goes on to add, "of feeling not strictly and necessarily connected with the passion." The meters move along in their own domain, scarcely intersecting the domain of meaning, except in some illusory fashion or by virtue of conventions nearly private. The responsibility they bear to the sense, comic writing aside, is mostly not to interfere. By so effacing themselves they will have accomplished all that they must accomplish in relation to the sense. Speech they can and do imitate, from a little distance, but rarely by quoting, that is to say, by attempting to become speech. Song they perhaps are or can become, their natural inclination: no question in that of imitating anything outside their own nature.

Whether their nature really embodies an imitation of natural processes may be arguable. But I do not think the meters can be, in any such sense, organic. A recognition of this, conscious or not, has been reason enough for their rejection by contemporary organicists, poets and critics both. The meters seem more to resemble the hammer-work of carpenters putting together a building, say, than waves coming in to shore or the parade of seasons. We do inhale and exhale more or less rhythmically, as long as we stay healthy; our

*Cf. Browning: I sprang to the stirrup, and Joris, and he;
   I galloped, Dirck galloped, we galloped all three.

hearts do beat without much skipping, for years on end. Breath and heart are the least remote of these similitudes, but any connection between them and the more or less regular alternation of weak and strong syllables in verse seems doubtful to me and, valid or not, need carry no particular prestige. In urban life, far from the Lake Country of 1800, are to be found analogies as appropriate as any from nature, if no more convincing. Signals timed to regulate the flow of traffic not only seem analogous but at times remarkably beautiful, as on a nearly deserted stretch of Ninth Avenue in New York City at three A.M., especially in a mild drizzle. If the meters do represent or imitate anything in general, it may be nothing more (or less) than some psychological compulsion, a sort of counting on the fingers or stepping on cracks, magic to keep an unpredictable world under control.

Where the meters are supposed to possess anything of an imitative character, the implicit purpose must be to bring the poetic text closer to its source in reality or nature by making it more "like" the thing it imitates. Such an illusion may be enhanced if the poet's conviction is strong enough to persuade an audience to share his faith, but such conversions are more likely to be accomplished through criticism than through poetry. The twin illusions of control and understanding seem more valuable to me than this illusion of the real, since it is through them, I suspect, that the meters are more firmly connected to memory. To remember an event is almost to begin to control it, as well as to approach an understanding of it; incapable of recurring now, it is only to be contemplated rather than acted on or reacted to. Any sacrifice of immediate reality is compensated for by these new perspectives. The terror or beauty or, for that matter, the plain ordinariness of the original event, being transformed, is fixed and thereby made more tolerable. That the event can recur only in its new context, the context of art, shears it of some risks, the chief of which may anyhow have been its transitory character.

If for an audience the meters function in part to call back the words of the poem, so for the poet they may help to call the words forth, at the same time casting over them the illusion of a necessary or at least not inappropriate fitness and order. There is a kind of accrediting in the process, a warrant that things are being remembered right and set down right, so long as the meters go on working. In this way the meters serve as a neutral and impersonal check on self-indulgence and whimsy; a subjective event gets made over into something more like an object. It becomes accessible to memory, repeatedly accessible, because it exists finally in a form that can be perused at leisure, like a snapshot in an album. Memory itself tends to act not without craft, but selectively, adding here to restore a gap, omitting the incongruous there, rearranging and shifting the emphasis, striving, consciously or not, to make some sense and point out of what in experience may have seemed to lack either. That other presence of which I spoke earlier—the charge of feeling, let us say, which attaches perhaps inexplicably to the subject, what the psychologist might call its *affect*—is not much subject to vicissitudes and manipulations of this sort, except for a natural enough diminution. It remains, but more than likely beneath the surface.

The meters are worth speculating about because they are so specific to the medium, if not altogether essential. Without them nothing may, on occasion, be lost; with them, on occasion, something may be gained, though whatever that is probably has little or nothing to do with sense or ostensible subject. This, in fact, appears to be the sticking point, that in themselves the meters signify so little. It seems a mistake for a rationalist defender of the meters to insist on too much meaningfulness. Let us concede that the effects of the meters are mysterious, from moment to moment imprecise, often enough uncertain or ambiguous. Like Coleridge's incense or wine, however, their presence may "act powerfully, though themselves unnoticed." To which he adds an interesting comparison to yeast—"worthless," as he says, "or disagreeable by itself, but giving vivacity and spirit to the liquor" in right combination. Meters do accompany the sense, like a kind of percussion only, mostly noise. Over and above syntax, they bind the individual words together, and the larger structural parts as well, over and above whatever appearance of logic survives in the argument; as a result, the words and parts seem to cohere, more perhaps than in plain fact may be the case. How they assist the recollection is by fixing it in permanent, or would-be permanent, form. This, for the poet, may be the large and rather sentimental purpose which gives force to all their various combining and intersecting functions.

The Invention of Free Verse

I MEAN by the invention of free verse only its invention in the twentieth century and in English. It had been invented in the nineteenth century in English by Whitman, in French by Laforgue (I would argue), and here and there even earlier in Western culture by apparent accident. But before our time free verse had not taken hold and swept the world before it.

The invention deserves commemoration. We must put up our plaque, however, not anywhere in New York or London, not even in Boston or Dublin, but in—unlikeliest of places—Crawfordsville, Indiana, somewhere in the environs of Wabash College. The year was 1907. The poet was more or less improvising, we may suppose, in the character of one of the old poets whom he had recently studied with such fondness and aptitude.

> Bah! I have sung women in three cities,
> But it is all the same;
> And I will sing of the sun.

Free verse has perhaps already been invented in these opening lines, but it is hard to be certain. Whatever is happening remains as yet undefined and indefinite. And it is at just this point that the poet, still in the assumed character of Cino, contrives an unmistakable little rhythmical motif, scarcely if ever heard before in English verse. (See end note.)

> Lips, words, and you snare them.

Note the two stresses brought together. This is the main point of the motif, after which comes the pair of slack syllables, as contrast perhaps or balance. What this arrangement of stressed and slack syllables resembles is the so-called ionic or double foot, as described by Ransom, among others, but it is not really quite the same, as Pound will prove only a moment later by way of variations played upon this base, variations extraordinarily difficult or impossible to arrange for in traditional practice, in anything outside of Hopkins's sprung rhythm, for that matter—and Hopkins's manuscripts were not to be published for yet another decade. No doubt that a cadence has here been found, beyond Tennyson, beyond Henley and Symons and Dowson, beyond Yeats. It may be taken as a test case of sorts. The proof will lie in whether the effect can be produced again, thus demonstrating that what has just taken place was not by chance.

> Lips, words, and you snare them,
> Dreams, words, and they are as jewels.

In theory it could be done; in practice it now has been done. The rest is mere elaboration and confirmation. For Pound himself the experience must have been like what the scientist undergoes in his laboratory, not altogether sure yet what he has or whether he has anything at all. The retorts, in any case, are bubbling. What joy in continuing, quite rapidly now, as I imagine.

> Lips, words, and you snare them,
> Dreams, words, and they are as jewels,
> Strange spells of old deity,
> Ravens, nights, allurement:
> And they are not;
> Having become the souls of song.

And if two stresses could be brought together, why not three? From "Ravens, nights, allurement" only let the slack syllables be dropped.

> Eyes, dreams, lips, and the night goes.
> Being upon the road once more,
> They are not.

The extension of "Lips, words" into "Eyes, dreams, lips" comes as the final confirmation that something has indeed taken place.

After the brilliance of this passage the poem lapses into a more typical early Pound pastiche, mannered and just barely post-nineties. The moment is finished. On the other hand, as we can see now, it was only a beginning.

Little of the free verse that was to follow has, it is true, anything much to do with this exact rhythmical motif, but I would maintain, even so, that here the iamb was first broken in a way decisive for twentieth-century poetry, decisive in large part of course because of Pound's own future development of the possibilities opened by this small first stroke of his. And even after the passing of so many decades there is still on these nine lines from "Cino" the shine of *the first time*.

End note: Other passages for comparison.

> Break, break, break,
> On thy cold grey stones, O Sea!
>
> —Tennyson, "Break, Break, Break," c. 1833.

> Hush, the Dead March wails in the people's ears:
> The dark crowd moves, and there are sobs and tears:
> The black earth yawns: the mortal disappears;
> Ashes to ashes, dust to dust;
> He is gone who seem'd so great.
>
> —Tennyson, "Ode on the Death of the Duke of Wellington," 1853.

> Shoulders and loins
> Ache---!
> Ache, and the mattress,
> Run into bolders and hummocks,
> Glows like a kiln, while the bedclothes—
> Tumbling, importunate, daft—
> Ramble and roll. . . .
>
> —Henley, "In Hospital," 1873–75.

> The sour scythe cringe, and the blear share come.
>
> —Hopkins, "The Wreck of the Deutschland," 1876 [published 1918].

> Wilt thóu glíde on the blue Pacific, or rest.
>
> —Bridges, "A Passer-by," 1879. [The accent marks are the poet's.]

It has been said of the Tennyson passages that they echo the funeral march from Handel's *Saul*, and it is certainly possible that the source of the cadence in Tennyson is somehow musical. It appears to connect for him with emotions associated with death and loss. For Pound, too, a specific musical source is at least possible, though less likely, I think, and any local emotional associations are clearly different for him than for Tennyson. Music is worth mentioning in this connection because of Auden's suggestion that keeping to the rhythms of specific musical texts can lead to metrical freshness and innovation. And it may be worth speculating about the emotional associations of a particular rhythmical motif, since links between emotion and rhythm often come up in theory. ["I believe in an 'absolute rhythm,' a rhythm, that is, in poetry which corresponds exactly to the emotion or shade of emotion to be expressed."—Pound.]

The Henley passage is for one instant virtually identical in movement to the Pound motif (lines 2 and 3 above) and is the closest parallel I have been able to turn up. It hardly seems a serious source, all the same, for Pound's invention.

The Prose Sublime:
Or, the Deep Sense of Things Belonging Together, Inexplicably

T H E R E must be in prose many passages capable of producing a particular kind of esthetic reaction more commonly identified with poetry. Unlike the classical sublime of Longinus, the prose sublime I have in mind would only in the simplest case depend for its effect on images or fine language; and those purple passages which, because they do so, are generally singled out for notice need not much concern us. In any case, the reaction to prose as to poetry proves in experience to be much the same, a sort of transport, a frisson, a thrilled recognition, which, "flashing forth at the right moment," as Longinus has it, "scatters everything before it like a thunderbolt."

In respect to poetry more than one effort has been made to pin down the very physiology of this reaction, albeit too personal and eccentric to be taken as universal. The report goes that Dickinson would feel, physically, as if the top of her head were taken off; her whole body grew so cold it seemed no fire could ever warm it. Housman's testimony is more circumstantial still. His skin, as he shaved, might bristle so that the razor ceased to act; a shiver would run down his spine or he would feel "a constriction of the throat and a precipitation of water to the eyes"; or something might go through him like a spear, and the seat of that particular sensation was "the pit of the stomach." We might suppose that physical sensations so violent and, it would seem, verging on the pathological would be enough to discourage all reading, but it is not so. We ourselves may have been spared the specific symptoms, but the remarkable similarity of such accounts remains impressive. Perhaps this much could be said, that some sense of elevation or elation may be felt which does not, for every reader, register itself in terms so physical. All the same, the illusion of something physical may be left behind, a shadow or tint not unlike the spreading of a blush, a suffusion of something warm and flowing just beneath the surface. Has not everyone felt something of the kind? The cool-minded R. P. Blackmur admits to "moods when the mere movement of words in pattern turns the shudder of recognition into a blush and the blush into vertigo." But however such feelings should be described matters less than the question of what it is that calls them forth.

The obvious place to look is just where everyone has always looked, in a prose which depends for its power primarily on the quality and distinction of its language. For there can be no doubt that fine prose of itself can and does give pleasure, and pleasure of the very kind to which poetry is normally thought to have first claim. The type of prose generally offered by way of example, however, would compromise the purity of the inquiry—prose that aims to be poetical: Pater or Doughty, perhaps, or self-consciously experimental work like *Tender Buttons* or *Finnegans Wake*. What this says of general ideas about poetry is too embarrassing and Victorian to pause over. We must try to find what we are looking for in a prose that does not aspire to the condition of poetry but is content to remain itself. Let us consider a passage not excessively familiar, one to which nothing of story and almost nothing of character can be adduced to explain its success: a specimen of prose pure and simple.

In the spring mornings I would work early while my wife still slept. The windows were open wide and the cobbles of the street were drying after the rain. The sun was drying the wet faces of the houses that faced the window. The shops were still shuttered. The goatherd came up the street blowing his pipes and a woman who lived on the floor above us came out onto the sidewalk with a big pot. The goatherd chose one of the heavy-bagged, black milk-goats and milked her into the pot while his dog pushed the others onto the sidewalk. The goats looked around, turning their necks like sight-seers. The goatherd took the money from the woman and thanked her and went on up the street piping and the dog herded the goats on ahead, their horns bobbing. I went back to writing and the woman came up the stairs with the goat milk. She wore her felt-soled cleaning shoes and I only heard her breathing as she stopped on the stairs outside our door and then the shutting of her door. She was the only customer for goat milk in our building.

Intense clarity: one-dimensional—everything rendered on a single plane. Whatever beauty the passage has—and it has as much as any passage of this scope can probably bear—depends less on the words themselves and the care taken with them than on this very sense that great care is in fact being taken. This leads to a strong sense of

the author's presence as manifested in the style, a style that seems
to come directly from the character of the author and is, practically
speaking, indistinguishable from it. With Hemingway this sense of
the author is rarely, if ever, absent, but that is just the point.
The author here would be felt as present even without the per-
sonal pronoun. He is present in the weight of the words picked out
and the rhythms of the composed and modeled phrases, as much as
in the attitudes and affectations of the Hemingwayesque. To pick up
A Moveable Feast for the first time, as I did not long ago, years after
its original publication, was to be astonished all over again, as in ado-
lescence, by the prose. I found myself content to read through it as if
it had no subject, as though the malicious gossip and tall tales were
nothing more than an excuse for the exercise of the famous muscular
style. The old I. A. Richards distinction between tenor and vehicle
seemed to reverse itself. The subject had become mere vehicle; the
true tenor—that is to say, what was being articulated by means of
all the beautiful, fierce detail—turned out to be the style itself.

Of course that is exaggeration. Yet if the prose sublime is here
at all, it seems lodged first in this way of using language and only
then, though inseparably, in the picture this language brings into
such clear and changeless focus. Technically speaking, this may in
some sense always be true or partly true, but it is rarely so decisively
true as here, and this rarity in itself becomes a factor in the reader's
admiration.

But beneath the surfaces of language, beyond even style or Black-
mur's "mere movement of words in pattern," there must be other
deeper and more hidden sources for the mysterious yet familiar feel-
ings we are trying to trace. A certain idealizing tendency in the criti-
cism of the past might lead us to assume that the most fundamental
source of all would lie in what James calls a "deep-breathing econ-
omy and an organic unity"; but in practice no example can ever be
adequate to the task of representing that. I must doubt, in any case,
whether an organic unity can be maintained except by an uncritical
assertion of faith and, as for economy, what we instead constantly
find ourselves overwhelmed by in novels is just the generosity of their
wastefulness. Often enough the reasons for what comes through as
the richest life and most sounding harmony in novels never do be-
come clear, though with our favorite authors we learn to trust that
somehow, anyhow, everything must, in a sense, belong. When the

reasons do too obtrusively loom up, it is right to suspect that some scheme of the author's is being imposed upon the reader.

According to Percy Lubbock, James's great interpreter, the reader of a novel finds it impossible to retain what Lubbock calls "the image of a book" entire. It must be nearly as hard for the author to manage this trick himself. Always, says Lubbock, "the image escapes and evades us like a cloud." Yet it does not entirely escape. In our memory there remains forever some image of the novel called *Madame Bovary*, and it is not at all the same as the remembered image of *War and Peace* or *The Wings of the Dove*. Ours are doubtless only phantasmal images of the whole—we could never, like a Borgesian character, become the true author of any of these novels—but these cloudy images have still enough of the contours of a wholeness about them to enable us to think of each one individually and quite distinctly.

And is wholeness the question anyhow? More vivid and alive, certainly, are those broken-off pieces of the whole which continue to drift across our consciousness more or less permanently, fragments though they are. In novels these pieces had once figured as scenes or the mere details of scenes; or as characters, characters in the end perhaps independent of the acts by which we had come to know them; or sometimes, though rarely, as a mere phrase or formula: "Hurrah for Karamazov!" Aside from whatever cloudy sense of the whole the reader may have held onto, such pieces are pretty much all that is left to prize, and there need be no embarrassment in conceding this simple truth.

I have said enough to indicate my belief that it would be futile to seek out the prose sublime in any large idea of artistic unity. Such ideas come to seem, in the light of experience, artificial, faintly theological. Even with the old Coleridgean formula—*unity in variety*—it might be well to emphasize, for a change, the uncanonized term of the pair, *variety*. For one form of the esthetic reaction we are trying to understand seems to occur just at that point when we grow aware that an ever-present and powerful sense of variety has begun to yield to what may never become more than a provisional sense of unity. A number of different things being put more or less together, one after the other, circling, recurring, veering off, they are seen to make a fit, perhaps quite unexpectedly, to be parts of some larger but undefinable complex. There comes over us then a deep sense of things belonging together, inexplicably. Joyce's "basic patterns are universal," observes Blackmur, "and are known without their names." Universal patterns concern me less than patterns of the occasion and, indeed, of so many changing occasions, if we had the time to look for them, that we could never expect to invent names to cover them all. Something of the mystery in the act of recognition, at which Blackmur hints, is probably always present.

There is a pattern familiar in modern poetry that may point to a similar, if less obvious, pattern in prose. It involves the simple juxtaposition of seemingly unrelated things. Take Pound's "In a Station of the Metro."

> The apparition of these faces in the crowd;
> Petals on a wet, black bough.

A rather high degree of likeness, based here on visual resemblance, is clearly intended, but the connection is never stated as such. It is a disposition of objects or perceptions, or of objects taking the place of perceptions, that is found here and there in Chinese poetry as well, a type of parataxis in which the implication of likeness is carried by the arrangement itself.* Nor should the expository importance of Pound's title escape notice; it forms the bottom note of a triad, so to speak, the three notes of which are set vibrating together in a new chord. To register, further, the social and emotional distance between a modern urban Metro station and the timeless pastoral of petal and bough is to see how the poem offers one more version of what Dr. Johnson long ago described as the "discovery of occult resemblances in things apparently unlike."

If we examine now a passage in prose, a long paragraph which likewise involves "things apparently unlike," we may catch something of the same pattern in action, though here less plainly laid out and therefore more elusive. The paragraph comes from the novel *Poor White*, by Sherwood Anderson, and it is chosen because, being unfamiliar, it has a chance to show freshly whatever force it may have. It is no more than a broken-off piece of a whole, but a whole in this case that really cannot be said to exist, a novel which survives, if it does, only in pieces, perhaps by now only in this very piece.

---

*A line from Li Po, cited in Wai-lim Yip's *Chinese Poetry*: "Floating cloud(s): wanderer's mood." Pound calls the arrangement, or something like it, "planes in relation."

Anderson seems never to have had a thought longer than thirty pages or so, and in the novel this paragraph rises toward whatever life and beauty it possesses out of a context truly flat and torpid. The plot is not important; there is practically no plot anyhow; Anderson did not like plot.

And then in Turner's Pike something happened.* A farmer boy, who had been to town and who had the daughter of a neighbor in his buggy, stopped in front of the house. A long freight train, grinding its way slowly past the station, barred the passage along the road. He held the reins in one hand and put the other about the waist of his companion. The two heads sought each other and lips met. They clung to each other. The same moon that shed its light on Rose McCoy in the distant farmhouse lighted the open place where the lovers sat in the buggy in the road. Hugh had to close his eyes and fight to put down an almost overpowering physical hunger in himself. His mind still protested that women were not for him. When his fancy made for him a picture of the school teacher Rose McCoy sleeping in a bed, he saw her only as a chaste white thing to be worshiped from afar and not to be approached, at least not by himself. Again he opened his eyes and looked at the lovers whose lips still clung together. His long slouching body stiffened and he sat up very straight in his chair. Then he closed his eyes again. A gruff voice broke the silence. "That's for Mike," it shouted and a great chunk of coal thrown from the train bounded across the potato patch and struck against the back of the house. Downstairs he could hear old Mrs. McCoy getting out of bed to secure the prize. The train passed and the lovers in the buggy sank away from each other. In the silent night Hugh could hear the regular beat of the hoofs of the farmer boy's horse as it carried him and his woman away into the darkness.

Perhaps we must be told that the railwaymen have worked up a custom of tossing out chunks of coal for the widow McCoy as they pass—times are hard; but we should be able to guess that Rose and Hugh, vague longings aside, are fated never to get together. Something of all this is probably implicit in the tone of the passage, in the emotional sense the scene does in its own way make. Yet it would be hard to find in these "things apparently unlike" very much that we could call resemblance, occult or not. Not everything is reducible to metaphor; there is more to our search than the uncovering of hidden likenesses. The mind recognizes readily enough how the parts

*To identify: Hugh is the dreamy, inarticulate hero; Rose McCoy is his landlady's schoolteacher daughter, who boards elsewhere; Mrs. McCoy is the widow of a railwayman named Mike; and Turner's Pike is a road leading out of a small midwestern town about the turn of the century.

of a poetic image fit together—often enough just the two halves of it, side by side—but in prose there is ampler room for maneuver. Any mixing of contraries may stop short of parallel or symmetry; it is the mere act of combining that seems to make the figure. Two or more things being put into play together are found, as by a sort of grace, to coexist somewhat harmoniously. In the Anderson passage the testing moment when this must be recognized or missed arrives with the chunk of coal, which has nothing whatever in common with moonlight or lovers in a buggy. The point is not just that the author states no connection; neither is any particular likeness implied, and it is in just this way that its pattern, if it has one, is markedly different from the Metro Station pattern. There is only the sentence in which the discord is resolved: "The train passed and the lovers in the buggy sank away from each other." The experience has the character of a ceremonial, small mystery; and I would add that what we experience seems to involve a perception of time. It is a classic instance of things coming together even as they pass, of a moment when things may be said to associate without relating. The feeling raised by this perception is one of poignancy; perhaps that is the specific feeling this type of the prose sublime can be expected to give rise to. Made up of unspoken connections, it seems also to be about them. Probably it is not peculiarly American, but I can recall nothing in European novels, not even in the Russians, which evokes and gives body to this particular mood.*

This may come in the end to nothing but one more attempt to deal with what is after all inexpressible. Yet something remains. Incidentally, no one can have read through many pages of Anderson without having been struck by the frequency in his prose of this word *something*: "And then in Turner's Pike something happened." The quintessential predicament for any character in Anderson is this: he (or she) wanted something and did not know what it was. It may be the universal predicament, for that matter. In any case, it resembles the predicament the reader of Anderson finds himself in, for he sees and seems almost to understand something without knowing what it is. Not that this feeling is brought about only by the sort of pattern we have been considering; it is rather that such a pattern can, like

*A more complicated and sustained example, again from forgotten Anderson, is Chapter 12 of his *Dark Laughter*, but it is far too long to quote here, and there are other problems.

patterns more clearly universal, also be known, though without its name, for indeed it has none.

In a brilliant essay entitled "Techniques of Fiction," Allen Tate refers to what he calls the "actuality" of a scene in *Madame Bovary*. It is the scene in which Emma, having received a letter of farewell from her lover, dashes up to the attic in a panic; there the sound of her neighbor Binet's lathe turning comes to her; the sound seems to draw her down toward the street, toward the death she already halfway desires. It is this purely coincidental detail of the lathe, which in no foreseeable way has anything to do with Emma's fate, that confers the sense of "actuality" on the scene for Tate. What he calls "actuality" is only a more philosophical or theological way of designating the esthetic moment when things associate powerfully together without apparent reason. Others have used the term "dramatic correlative" for such a connecting, an echo no doubt of Eliot's "objective correlative." Presumably the novelist, by identifying the process, might make use of it at will, though I do not find it mentioned as a device in the pages of *The Rhetoric of Fiction*. Nor in the Anderson passage is any sense of actuality it happens to possess so much built up and managed as it is simply taken for granted, either naively or confidently—rather, let us say, with the very confidence which can be one of the great assets of the naive writer.

Such moments are akin to the Joycean epiphany or to the "frozen pictures" of novels, moments at which the action, pausing, gives way to a held picture, something like the cinematic freeze-frame or a fermata in music; the picture in itself seems to represent, almost abstractly, some complex of meaning and feeling.* When Prince Andrey, wounded, looks up at the "lofty" and "limitless" sky, the effect is of a kind of summation, the meaning of which can be and, as it happens, is stated: "Yes, all is vanity, all is a cheat, except that infinite sky." The Joycean epiphany seems likewise to be a form of revelation or insight; the meaning in wait around the last turned corner of narrative is suddenly illuminated by a flash of understanding: "Gazing up into the darkness I saw myself as a creature driven and derided by vanity; and my eyes burned with anguish and anger." This is very beautifully said, and we may for a moment wonder, as Longinus might have wondered, if the effect is not grounded in the

*Stage tableaux work a little in this way, especially at curtains, though a sense of contrivance can compromise the purity of the effect.

flash of style as much as in the flash of understanding; yet both are present.

In Anderson there is not the same push toward meaning; the rendering exhausts the interpretation: "The train passed and the lovers in the buggy sank away from each other." This has everything the Joycean epiphany has except for the crucial flash of understanding; and the plain style of it I find quite unofficially beautiful as well. Such a passage seems hardly to bother with understanding at all; it is a passage of unspoken connections, unnameable affinities, a tissue of association without specified relations. As far as I know, this last species of the prose sublime, being so elusive, has not previously been isolated and identified.

In it, connections, if any, remain unstated; likewise meanings. As used to be remarked of poems, such passages resist paraphrase. Their power is hidden in mystery. There is, at most, an illusion of seeing momentarily into the heart of things—and the moment vanishes. It is this, perhaps, which produces the esthetic blush.

Notes

"Henry James by the Pacific." In March 1905, James stayed at the Hotel del Coronado near San Diego.

"Chorus" and "Epilogue: To the Morning Light." *Bad Dreams*, the unfinished long poem from which these two poems come, was to have been made up mostly of dreams dreamed by the kinspeople gathered in the house of the head of the family on the night he lay dying. Some debt for the idea is doubtless owed to James Agee and Peter Taylor, but I can no longer judge how much.

"Memories of the Depression Years." 2 (Boston, Georgia) is a kind of *imitation* of the Wang Wei poem, which has been translated as "A Farmhouse on the Wei River." 3 (Miami, Florida) bears a similar relation to Baudelaire's *Je n'ai pas oublié . . .*

"Childhood." Line 2: Czechoslovakia, e.g. Line 5: The "Katzenjammer Kids" were for years the feature comic strip of the Sunday *Miami Herald*. Lines 23–26: The Olympia Theater. Lines 32ff.: The hurricane season. Line 37: An obsolete make of car. Lines 38–39: The Everglades on fire. Lines 40ff.: My osteomyelitis and the anesthesias it involved. Lines 44–45: The Capitol Barber Shop, M. DuPree, proprietor. Lines 46–47: Billy's Men's Shop. Lines 49–50: In Cromer-Cassell's (later Richards') Department Store. Lines 51–52: The segregated drinking fountains of those days. Lines 54ff.: The 5-and-10¢ stores. A tray of unsorted eyeglasses at Grant's. A toy display in Woolworth's. Lines 58ff.: The N.W. section, still under development. Line 69: Sunny Isles, Golden Glades, Buena Vista, Opa-Locka, etc.

"Hell." The speaker is Robert Boardman Vaughn. Line 6 is taken unchanged from "The Spell," a poem in his unpublished manuscript. Parts of the next few lines are freely adapted from another poem of his, "The Black Rose."

"Incident in a Rose Garden." The Somerset Maugham version, used by John O'Hara in his *Appointment in Samarra*, goes as follows:

DEATH SPEAKS: There was a merchant in Baghdad who sent his servant to market to buy provisions and in a little while the servant came back, white and trembling, and said, Master, just now when I was in the market-place I was jostled by a woman in the crowd and when I turned I saw it was Death that jostled me. She looked at me and made a threatening gesture; now, lend me your horse, and I will ride away from this city and avoid my fate. I will go to Samarra and there Death will not find me. The merchant lent him his horse, and the servant mounted it, and he dug his spurs in its flanks and as fast as the horse could gallop he went. Then the merchant went down to the market-place and he saw me standing in the crowd and he came to me and said, Why did you make a threatening gesture to my servant when you saw him this morning? That was not a threatening gesture, I said, it was only a start of surprise. I was astonished to see him in Bagdad, for I had an appointment with him tonight in Samarra.

"On a Painting by Patient B." B's names for the clouds were Rabbit, Bear, and Hyena.

"Sea-Wind: A Song" and "Last Evening: At the Piano." Rilke's poems date from the poet's stay in Capri early in 1907. My versions came out of an attempt to write a play loosely based on that period of the poet's life. The famous image of the death's-head shako with which "Letzer Abend" ends I have de-Prussianized, since in my play both poet and setting had become American.

"The Metamorphoses of a Vampire." Line 12 of the French text I was using reads *véloutés* rather than *rédoutés*.

"Young Girls Growing Up (1911)." See *The Diaries of Franz Kafka: 1910– 1913*, entries for November 29 and December 3.

"Variations on a Text by Vallejo." The Greek poet, Kostas Ouránis (1890– 1953), deserves some credit for this motif. Though I did not come across it until years after my own version, Ouránis has a poem apparently dating from 1915, the first line of which, in Kimon Friar's translation, reads: "I shall die one day on a mournful autumn twilight."

"Homage to the Memory of Wallace Stevens." The last section refers to a libretto I wrote for Edward Miller's opera, *The Young God*, to its per-formance, and to the accompanying celebrations, which took place in Hartford in the spring of 1969. Line 22 is meant to echo a famous line from "Lycidas."

"The Sunset Maker" and "Little Elegy for Cello and Piano." The musical quotation comes from a piece I wrote as a student of Carl Ruggles in 1943.

Acknowledgments

My grateful acknowledgments to the editors of the publications in which these heretofore uncollected pieces originally appeared:

"The Metamorphoses of a Vampire," *Reading Modern Poetry*, 1955.

"Chorus," *Poetry*, 1959.

"Porch [first poem in 'South']," *The Atlantic*, 1982.

"The Invention of Free Verse," *The Iowa Review*, 1985.

"The Prose Sublime," *Michigan Quarterly Review*, 1988.

"Dance Lessons of the Thirties," *The New Criterion*, 1988.

"On a Woman of Spirit Who Taught Both Piano and Dance," *The New Criterion*, 1989.

"Body and Soul," *Antaeus*, 1990.

"Monologue in an Attic," *Literary Outtakes*, 1990.

Printed in the United States
34759LVS00002B/88

9 780874 516265